STUDY GUIDE

INDIANA CHRISTIAN UNIVERSITY

DEMONOLOGY & DELIVERANCE

Principalities & Powers
Foundational Studies

Volume I

by
DR. LESTER SUMRALL

Sumrall Publishing
P.O. Box 12
South Bend, IN 46624

This special study guide is a college workbook. Space is prepared for your personal notes so the text can grow into your own material.

Audio and videotapes are available to assist you.

All scriptures, unless otherwise indicated, are taken from the *King James Version of the Holy Bible.*

DEMONOLOGY & DELIVERANCE I
ISBN 0-937580-54-6

Printed by Sumrall Publishing
P.O. Box 12
South Bend, Indiana 46624

STUDY GUIDE
INDIANA CHRISTIAN UNIVERSITY

DEMONOLOGY & DELIVERANCE I

TABLE OF CONTENTS

STUDY GUIDE

INDIANA CHRISTIAN UNIVERSITY

DEMONOLOGY & DELIVERANCE I

Lesson 1

INTRODUCTION TO DIVINE DELIVERANCE

READING:

1 Peter 5:8-9, *Be sober, be vigilant; because your adversary the devil, as a roaring lion, walketh about, seeking whom he may devour:*
v. 9, *Whom resist stedfast in the faith, knowing that the same afflictions are accomplished in your brethren that are in the world.*

1. THESE ARE POSSIBLY THE MOST PERTINENT LESSONS I HAVE EVER PREPARED

   These studies have to do with unnatural power and dominion over intelligent beings.

2. THE SCOPE OF THE STUDIES IS UNIVERSAL

   The devil has no respect for race, nation, or person.

3. THESE STUDIES ARE IMPERATIVE AT THIS POINT IN TIME

   Our world is rapidly and drastically changing. Our society is being attacked by occult forces. Magic is now having its greatest resurgence in modern history. Satanism is springing up in every city and town.

4. MANY CHURCH LEADERS ARE CONCERNED ABOUT OCCULTISM AND DEMON POWER TODAY

   A. Pope Paul said, "Whole societies have fallen under the domination of the devil. Sex and narcotics provide openings for Satan's infiltration of mankind.

One of the great needs of our time is a defense against the evil which we call the devil. We all are under an obscure domination. It is Satan, the prince of this world, the No. 1 enemy."

B. Billy Graham said, "The devil is actively engaged in combating America's growing religious revival. The proof of the devil's work is the increasing interest in the occult--including astrology, tarot-card readings, ouija boards, palmistry, fortune-telling, and particularly, witchcraft. It is perfectly obvious to all of us in spiritual work that people can be possessed by demons, harassed by them, and controlled by them. More and more ministers will have to learn to use the power of God to release people from these terrible possessions by the devil."

5. CHRISTIANS ARE BECOMING MORE AWARE OF THE INFLUENCE OF DEMONS

A. A few years ago those who took a stand against demons were criticized and not believed. That time is gone. Now Christians want information on how to discern demon power.

B. They want to know how to exorcise demons.

C. They also want to know how to keep people free from the influence of satanic forces. There are three known sources of energy in our universe.

Let's learn together . . .

Let's advance together . . . NOW!

STUDY GUIDE

INDIANA CHRISTIAN UNIVERSITY

DEMONOLOGY & DELIVERANCE I

Lesson 2

THE THREE SOURCES OF ENERGY

INTRODUCTION:

Our universe is no accident. It did not evolve through erratic and fortuitous forces of unknown origin. The functions and movements of the cosmic dimensions are intricate.

The unlimited and immeasurable galaxies of the heavenly bodies in outer space are vast. Our universe--of which planet Earth is a finite, yet very active part--is real, but it has been invaded by demonic forces.

READING:

Genesis 1:1, *In the beginning God created the heaven and the earth.*

1. THERE ARE THREE KNOWN INTELLIGENT SOURCES OF ENERGY IN OUR REALM OF KNOWLEDGE:

    A.   There is God's power.

    God is the creative and benevolent personality of the universe.

    Isaiah 64:8, . . .*O LORD, thou art our father; we are the clay, and thou our potter; and we all are the work of thy hand.*

    Acts 10:38, . . .*God anointed Jesus of Nazareth with the Holy Ghost and with power: who went about doing good, and healing all that were oppressed of the devil; for God was with him.*

    Hebrews 1:1, *GOD, who at sundry times and in divers manners spake in time past unto the fathers by the prophets,*

    B.   There is man's power.

Man is a neutral power with potential to become a part of the good or the bad power.

The Apostle Paul said to man in Romans 6:16, *Know ye not, that to whom ye yield yourselves servants to obey, his servants ye are to whom ye obey; whether of sin unto death, or of obedience unto righteousness?*

    C.   There is the devil's power.

The devil is a malevolent personality who seeks to destroy God's work and man's life. As a revolutionary, he upset the heavens. He collected angelic followers and they became fallen angels. (See Lesson 3. See Isaiah 14:12-14)

John 10:10, *The thief cometh not, but for to steal, and to kill, and to destroy: I am come that they might have life, and that they might have it more abundantly.*

The devil has caused the ills and sorrows of mankind from the Garden of Eden to this point in history. The devil works through fallen angels, men, or cosmic forces of nature to bring to pass his evil designs.

Job 1:19, *And, behold, there came a great wind from the wilderness, and smote the four corners of the house, and it fell upon the young men, and they are dead; and I only am escaped alone to tell thee.*

Mark 4:37-38, *And there arose a great storm of wind, and the waves beat into the ship, so that it was now full.*
v. 38, And he was in the hinder part of the ship, asleep on a pillow: and they awake him, and say unto him, Master, carest thou not that we perish?

2. THE HOLY SCRIPTURES

    A.   Satan is directly spoken of over 200 times in the Bible. In Genesis chapter three, Satan enters the realm of human activity.

Genesis 3:1-7, *Now the serpent was more subtil than any beast of the field which the LORD God had made. And he said unto the woman, Yea, hath God said, Ye shall not eat of every tree of the garden?*
v. 2, And the woman said unto the serpent, We may eat of the fruit of the trees of the garden:
v. 3, But of the fruit of the tree which is in the midst of the garden, God hath said, Ye shall not eat of it, neither shall ye touch it, lest ye die.
v. 4, And the serpent said unto the woman, Ye shall not surely die:
v. 5, For God doth know that in the day ye eat thereof, then your eyes shall be opened, and ye shall be as gods, knowing good and evil.

v. 6, *And when the woman saw that the tree was good for food, and that it was pleasant to the eyes, and a tree to be desired to make one wise, she took of the fruit thereof, and did eat, and gave also unto her husband with her; and he did eat.*

v. 7, *And the eyes of them both were opened, and they knew that they were naked; and they sewed fig leaves together, and made themselves aprons.*

B.   Job chapter one reveals that Satan is an oppressor of good people.

Job 1:9-12, *Then Satan answered the LORD, and said, Doth Job fear God for nought?*

v. 10, *Hast not thou made an hedge about him, and about his house, and about all that he hath on every side? thou hast blessed the work of his hands, and his substance is increased in the land.*

v. 11, *But put forth thine hand now, and touch all that he hath, and he will curse thee to thy face.*

v. 12, *And the LORD said unto Satan, Behold, all that he hath is in thy power; only upon himself put not forth thine hand. So Satan went forth from the presence of the LORD.*

C.   Matthew chapter four shows the audacity of the devil in tempting the Lord Jesus Christ.

Matthew 4:3, 6, 8, *And when the tempter came to him, he said, If thou be the Son of God, command that these stones be made bread.*

v. 6, *And saith unto him, If thou be the Son of God, cast thyself down: for it is written, He shall give his angels charge concerning thee: and in their hands they shall bear thee up, lest at any time thou dash thy foot against a stone.*

v. 8, *Again, the devil taketh him up into an exceeding high mountain, and sheweth him all the kingdoms of the world, and the glory of them.*

D.   Satan's final incarceration and eternal confinement are predicted in Revelation 20:10, *And the devil that deceived them was cast into the lake of fire and brimstone, where the beast and the false prophet are, and shall be tormented day and night for ever and ever.*

3.   THE DEVIL DOES NOT WANT THE TRUTH ABOUT HIMSELF DISCLOSED

He hates exposure of his deeds and camouflages himself as an angel of light.

2 Corinthians 11:14, *. . . for Satan himself is transformed into an angel of light.*

4. CHRISTIAN ACTION

The Christian is to take action against the devil.

Acts 8:17-24, *Then laid they their hands on them, and they received the Holy Ghost.*
v. 18, *And when Simon saw that through laying on of the apostles' hands the Holy Ghost was given, he offered them money.*
v. 19, *Saying, Give me also this power, that on whomsoever I lay hands, he may receive the Holy Ghost.*
v. 20, *But Peter said unto him, Thy money perish with thee, because thou hast thought that the gift of God may be purchased with money.*
v. 21, *Thou hast neither part nor lot in this matter: for thy heart is not right in the sight of God.*
v. 22, *Repent therefore of this thy wickedness, and pray God, if perhaps the thought of thine heart may be forgiven thee.*
v. 23, *For I perceive that thou art in the gall of bitterness, and in the bond of iniquity.*
v. 24, *Then answered Simon, and said, Pray ye to the Lord for me, that none of these things which ye have spoken come upon me.*

A. The Word of God warns that believers should give no place, no honor, no praise, and no fear to the devil.

Ephesians 4:27, *Neither give place to the devil.*

B. Followers of Christ must believe, accept, and obey the words of God-- defending the church and aggressively defeating Satan's designs upon mankind.

Matthew 16:18, *And I say also unto thee, That thou art Peter, and upon this rock I will build my church; and the gates of hell shall not prevail against it.*

C. The Christian must work with God to consummate the final destiny of the devil.

Revelation 20:10, *And the devil that deceived them was cast into the lake of fire and brimstone, where the beast and the false prophet are, and shall be tormented day and night for ever and ever.*

D. This is adversarial warfare. We are not to be ignorant of the devil's wiles.

I Peter 5:8-9, *Be sober, be vigilant; because your adversary the devil, as a roaring lion, walketh about, seeking whom he may devour:*
v. 9, *Whom resist stedfast in the faith, knowing that the same afflictions are accomplished in your brethren that are in the world.*

STUDY GUIDE

INDIANA CHRISTIAN UNIVERSITY

DEMONOLOGY & DELIVERANCE I

Lesson 3

THE ORIGIN OF SATAN

1. HIS ORIGIN AND IDENTITY

Fortunately we have the full story of the fall, the works, and the destiny of the devil in the Bible.

Ezekiel 28:12-19, *Son of man, take up a lamentation upon the king of Tyrus, and say unto him, Thus saith the Lord GOD; Thou sealest up the sum, full of wisdom, and perfect in beauty.*

v. 13, *Thou hast been in Eden the garden of God; every precious stone was thy covering, the sardius, topaz, and the diamond, the beryl, the onyx, and the jasper, the sapphire, the emerald, and the carbuncle, and gold: the workmanship of thy tabrets and of thy pipes was prepared in thee in the day that thou wast created.*

v. 14, *Thou art the anointed cherub that covereth; and I have set thee so: thou wast upon the holy mountain of God; thou hast walked up and down in the midst of the stones of fire.*

v. 15, *Thou wast perfect in thy ways from the day that thou wast created, till iniquity was found in thee.*

v. 16, *By the multitude of thy merchandise they have filled the midst of thee with violence, and thou hast sinned: therefore I will cast thee as profane out of the mountain of God: and I will destroy thee, O covering cherub, from the midst of the stones of fire.*

v. 17, *Thine heart was lifted up because of thy beauty, thou hast corrupted thy wisdom by reason of thy brightness: I will cast thee to the ground, I will lay thee before kings, that they may behold thee.*

v. 18, *Thou hast defiled thy sanctuaries by the multitude of thine iniquities, by the iniquity of thy traffic; therefore will I bring forth a fire from the midst of thee, it shall devour thee, and I will bring thee to ashes upon the earth in the sight of all them that behold thee.*

v. 19, *All they that know thee among the people shall be astonished at thee: thou shalt be a terror, and never shalt thou be any more.*

2. HIS FALL

He was a powerful angel who became perverted and rebelled against God, and became known as Satan and the devil. Note the five foolish and fatal "I wills" of Lucifer in these verses.

Isaiah 14:12-14, *How art thou fallen from heaven, O Lucifer, son of the morning! how art thou cut down to the ground, which didst weaken the nations!*
v. 13, *For thou hast said in thine heart, I will ascend into heaven, I will exalt my throne above the stars of God: I will sit also upon the mount of the congregation, in the sides of the north:*
v. 14, *I will ascend above the heights of the clouds; I will be like the most High.*

3. REBELLION IN PARADISE

Not content to be the beautiful, intelligent creature of God and of the highest order of angels, Satan aspired to a position of equality with God. His contest seems to have been most specifically with Jesus Christ, although the entire Godhead was challenged! This conflict has endured through the ages and will not be entirely consummated until Satan is cast into the lake of fire forever and ever.

Satan was created an archangel, the highest order of God's creation. This description in Ezekiel 28 can only be applied to a supernatural being and not a man who ruled Tyre.

Ezekiel 28:12, *Son of man, take up a lamentation upon the king of Tyrus, and say unto him, Thus saith the Lord GOD; Thou sealest up the sum, full of wisdom, and perfect in beauty.*

4. SATAN'S POWER

Satan's titles, his abilities, and his spheres of influence are clearly defined.

In Ezekiel 28:14, 16, Satan is called the cherub that covereth.

He is spoken of as walking up and down in the midst of the stones of fire.

Ezekiel 28:14, 16, *Thou art the anointed cherub that covereth; and I have set thee so: thou wast upon the holy mountain of God; thou hast walked up and down in the midst of the stones of fire.*

v. 16, *By the multitude of thy merchandise they have filled the midst of thee with violence, and thou hast sinned; therefore I will cast thee as profane out of the mountain of God: and I will destroy thee, O covering cherub, from the midst of the stones of fire.*

Fire is often used to speak of the presence of Jehovah: the burning bush, sacrificial fire, fire of incense, and pillar of fire.

Hebrews 12:29, *For our God is a consuming fire.*

Cherubs attended to the holiness of God.

In the Tabernacle and Temple, cherubs were represented by two golden figures of two winged living creatures. They covered the mercy seat in the Holy of Holies.

The first reference to the cherubim is in Genesis 3:24. Certain other Old Testament references give clear indication that angelic beings are upon occasion in view (Psalm 18:10; Ezekiel 28:4).

Exodus 25:20, *And the cherubims shall stretch forth their wings on high, covering the mercy seat with their wings, and their faces shall look one to another; toward the mercy seat shall the faces of the cherubims be.*

Satan was "the anointed cherub" or *mimshach* in the Hebrew language. It is used but once in the Old Testament and signifies outspreading, as of wings.

5. SATAN WAS BEAUTIFUL

He must have been a gorgeous creature to look upon. He fell through pride over his personal beauty. His own clothing was "covered" with the most costly of stones.

Ezekiel 28:12-13, *Son of man, take up a lamentation upon the king of Tyrus, and say unto him, Thus saith the Lord GOD; Thou sealest up the sum, full of wisdom, and perfect in beauty.*
v. 13, *Thou hast been in Eden the garden of God; every precious stone was thy covering, the sardius, topaz, and the diamond, the beryl, the onyx, and the jasper, the sapphire, the emerald, and the carbuncle, and gold: the workmanship of thy tabrets and of thy pipes was prepared in thee in the day that thou wast created .*

Eden, his headquarters, was a paradise. He is spoken of as walking up and down in the midst of the stones of fire.

6. MELODY AND MUSIC

Your heart was lifted up because of your beauty; You corrupted your wisdom for the sake of your splendor. . .(NKJV).

Here is the first sin--the sin of pride. The Bible clearly teaches in Proverbs 16:18, *Pride goes before destruction, and a haughty spirit before a fall (AMP).* Pride is a destroyer.

Ezekiel 28:13, . . . *The workmanship of your timbrels and pipes was prepared for you on the day you were created* (NKJV).

This accounts for the tremendous use of music Satan makes today, damning souls through music when he used to lead praise to God with music. Dr. J. Dwight Pentecost has written: "Musical instruments were originally designed to be means of praising and worshipping God. It was not necessary for Lucifer to learn to play a musical instrument in order to praise God. If you please, he had a built-in pipe organ, or, he was an organ. That's what the prophet meant when he said 'the workmanship of thy tabrets and of thy pipes. . .' Lucifer, because of his beauty, did what a musical instrument would do in the hands of a skilled musician, bring forth a paean of praise to the glory of God. Lucifer didn't have to look for someone to play the organ so that he would sing the doxology--he was the doxology!" (From *Your Adversary, the Devil,* pg. 16).

7. FROM AN ANGEL TO A DEVIL

Satan fell through pride over his personal beauty. Pride is a destroyer.

Ezekiel 28:17, *Your heart was lifted up because of your beauty; You corrupted your wisdom for the sake of your splendor; I cast you to the ground, I laid you before kings, That they might gaze at you* (NKJV).

Satan's greed and lust of physical and material things supplanted his spiritual service to Jehovah.

Ezekiel 28:16, *By the abundance of your trading you became filled with violence within, and you sinned; Therefore I cast you as a profane thing out of the mountain of God; And I destroyed you, O covering cherub, from the midst of the fiery stones* (NKJV).

The multitude of Lucifer's possessions lifted his heart with pride. These have been his major tools in tempting men into sin ever since--pride of possession and pride of physical beauty. If these things could produce iniquity in the "cherub that covereth" how easily will they produce iniquity in sinful flesh like ours!

In the New Testament, the Apostle John warned believers to be aware of three deadly temptations. These are (1) the lust of the flesh, (2) the lust of the eyes, and (3) the pride of life. See 1 John 2:15-17.

In the Garden, Satan subjected Eve to all three. Satan was well acquainted, as this Ezekiel passage shows, with these lusts. They caused his own downfall.

8. STILL A DIGNITARY

In Jude verse 9 we read that Michael (an archangel, a person of great power and position in heaven) refused to rebuke Satan in the dispute over Moses' body. Even in his fallen state, Satan is still one of the greatest and keenest personalities ever created.

Jude 9, *Yet Michael the archangel, in contending with the devil when he disputed about the body of Moses, dared not bring against him a reviling accusation, but said, "The Lord rebuke you!"* (NKJV).

9. LUCIFER, THE DEVIL, IS A REAL PERSON

The devil is not an influence or an idea or an abstract design. He is a person.

I Peter 5:8, *Be sober, be vigilant; because your adversary the devil, as a roaring lion, walketh about, seeking whom he may devour.*

A. Personal names and titles are given to him.

   Revelation 20:2, *And he laid hold on the dragon, that old serpent, which is the Devil, and Satan, and bound him a thousand years.* (For more on this refer to Lesson 6)

B. Personal acts and characteristics are ascribed to him.

   Isaiah 14:12-15, *How art thou fallen from heaven, O Lucifer, son of the morning! how art thou cut down to the ground, which didst weaken the nations!*
   v. 13, *For thou hast said in thine heart, I will ascend into heaven, I will exalt my throne above the stars of God: I will sit also upon the mount of the congregation, in the sides of the north:*
   v. 14, *I will ascend above the heights of the clouds; I will be like the most High.*
   v. 15, *Yet thou shalt be brought down to hell, to the sides of the pit.*

C. Jesus dealt with the devil as a person.

   Matthew 4:8-10, *Again, the devil taketh him up into an exceeding high mountain, and sheweth him all the kingdoms of the world, and the glory of them;*
   v. 9, *And saith unto him, All these things will I give thee, If thou wilt fall down and worship me.*
   v. 10, *Then saith Jesus unto him, Get thee hence, Satan: for it is written, Thou shalt worship the Lord thy God, and him only shalt thou serve.*

    D.   Jesus waged war on Satan as on a person.

        Luke 13:16, *And ought not this woman, being a daughter of Abraham, whom Satan hath bound, lo, these eighteen years, be loosed from this bond on the sabbath day?*

    E.   Paul, in the epistles, gave instruction on dealing with Satan as with a real person. Paul himself waged war on Satan many times.

        Ephesians 6:10-12, *Finally, my brethren, be strong in the Lord, and in the power of his might.*
        v. 11, *Put on the whole armour of God, that ye may be able to stand against the wiles of the devil.*
        v. 12, *For we wrestle not against flesh and blood, but against principalities, against powers, against the rulers of the darkness of this world, against spiritual wickedness in high places.*

    F.   The devil has been spoken of as possessing personal characteristics; a heart, pride, speech, knowledge, power, desires, and lusts.

STUDY GUIDE

INDIANA CHRISTIAN UNIVERSITY

DEMONOLOGY & DELIVERANCE I

Lesson 4

THE ORIGIN OF DEMONS

INTRODUCTION:

The word "demons" is not in the King James Version of the Bible, but their existence is evident and other versions and translations use the word.

The Bible teaches that apart from Satan, the prince and power of the air, there exist evil spirits of lesser degree of leadership and power. Their designation as demons is from the Greek word *diabolos*, meaning "adversary, false accuser, and slanderer," and from the Latin word *daemon*, meaning "evil spirit."

1. THE ORIGIN OF DEMONS

In Satan's rebellion in heaven he drew with him a great multitude of lesser celestial beings.

Revelation 12:4, *And his tail drew the third part of the stars of heaven, and did cast them to the earth. . .* (see also Ezekiel 28 and Isaiah 14 for further reference).

These are called "the devil's angels."

Matthew 25:41, *Then shall he say also unto them on the left hand, Depart from me, ye cursed, into everlasting fire, prepared for the devil and his angels.*

These unconfined, wicked spirits are under Satan's kingdom and dominion. They are his emissaries and subjects and are so numerous they make his power practically unlimited.

2. THE NATURE OF DEMONS

A.   Demons are personalities, as humans are personalities.

B.   A human is a personality with a corporate body.

C.   Demons are personalities without corporate existence. They cannot be seen with mortal eyes. As fallen spirits, they desire to dwell in a body in order to manifest themselves. Throughout God's Word, we find these evil spirits indwelling human bodies. Fallen spirits are essentially and irretrievably evil, malevolent creatures. They are angry with God because they lost their estate in heaven. Their prime motive is to destroy what God loves or creates. Since God loves the human race more than anything else, they wish to hurt and destroy it. When one becomes a believer and a militant Christian, then a constant warfare begins with Satan.

3.   THE ABODE OF DEMONS

Satan's methods of activity and his highly organized empire of roving spirits in the heavenlies are recorded in Ephesians 6:12, *For we wrestle not against flesh and blood, but against principalities, against powers, against the rulers of the darkness of this world, against spiritual wickedness in high places.*

His methods are suggested by the expression "wiles of the devil" (see Ephesians 6:11). His organization is graduated, containing principalities, powers, world rulers of this darkness, and spiritual hosts of wickedness in high places. It is in the heavenlies above the earth that the devil and his angels, or demons, have their abode and base of operation.

4.   JESUS TAUGHT THE EXISTENCE OF DEMONS

Jesus mentioned Satan at least fifteen times and taught the existence of demons.

A.   He cast them out of people.

Matthew 15:22-33, *And, behold, a woman of Canaan came out of the same coasts, and cried unto him, saying, Have mercy on me, O Lord, thou Son of David; my daughter is grievously vexed with a devil.*
v. 23, *But he answered her not a word. And his disciples came and besought him, saying, Send her away; for she crieth after us.*
v. 24, *But he answered and said, I am not sent but unto the lost sheep of the house of Israel.*
v. 25, *Then came she and worshipped him, saying, Lord, help me.*
v. 26, *But he answered and said, It is not meet to take the children's bread, and to cast it to dogs.*
v. 27, *And she said, Truth, Lord: yet the dogs eat of the crumbs which fall from their masters' table.*
v. 28, *Then Jesus answered and said unto her, O woman, great is thy faith: be it unto thee even as thou wilt. And her daughter was made whole from that very hour.*

B.   He commanded His disciples to cast them out.

Matthew 10:1, *And when he had called unto him his twelve disciples, he gave them power against unclean spirits, to cast them out, and to heal all manner of sickness and all manner of disease.*

Mark 16:17, *And these signs shall follow them that believe; In my name shall they cast out devils; they shall speak with new tongues.*

Luke 9:1, *Then he called his twelve disciples together, and gave them power and authority over all devils, and to cure diseases.*

5.   THE APOSTLES BELIEVED IN THE EXISTENCE OF DEMONS

The apostles believed firmly in the existence of demons.

A.   Matthew suggested their origin under Satan.

Matthew 12:26, *And if Satan castout Satan, he is divided against himself. How then will his kingdom stand?* (NKJV).

B.   Matthew spoke of their final doom.

Matthew 25:41, *Then He will also say to those on the left hand, Depart from Me, you cursed, into the everlasting fire prepared for the devil and his angels.*

C.   Luke described their nature, their expulsion from heaven, and their place of dwelling.

Luke 4:33, *And in the synagogue there was a man, which had a spirit of an unclean devil, and cried out with a loud voice.*

Luke 6:18, *And they that were vexed with unclean spirits: and they were healed.*

Luke told of their expulsion from human beings.

Luke 9:42, *And as he was still coming, the demon threw him down and convulsed him. Then Jesus rebuked the unclean spirit, healed the child, and gave him back to his father* (NKJV).

Luke told of their place of dwelling.

Luke 8:27-33, *And when He stepped out on the land, there met Him a certain man from the city who had demons for a long time. And he wore no clothes, nor did he live in a house but in the tombs.*
v. 28, *When he saw Jesus, he cried out, fell down before Him, and with a loud voice said, What have I to do with you, Jesus, Son of the Most High God?*

v. 29, *For He had commanded the unclean spirit to come out of the man. For it had often seized him, and he was kept under guard, bound with chains and shackles, and he broke the bonds and was driven by the demon into the wilderness.*

v. 30, *Jesus asked him, saying, What is your name? And he said, Legion, because many demons had entered him.*

v. 31, *And they begged Him that He would not command them to go out into the abyss.*

v. 32, *Now a herd of many swine was feeding there on the mountain. And they begged Him that He would permit them to enter them. And He permitted them.*

v. 33, *Then the demons went out of the man and entered the swine, and the herd ran violently down the steep place into the lake and drowned* (NKJV).

D.   Paul, in writing to Timothy, warned him of the "doctrine of devils." The writer of Revelation did the same.

I Timothy 4:1, *Now the Spirit speaketh expressly, that in the latter times some shall depart from the faith, giving heed to seducing spirits, and doctrines of devils.*

Revelation 16:14, *For they are the spirits of devils, working miracles, which go forth unto the kings of the earth and of the whole world, to gather them to the battle of the great day of God Almighty.*

STUDY GUIDE

INDIANA CHRISTIAN UNIVERSITY

DEMONOLOGY & DELIVERANCE I

Lesson 5

NAMES THE BIBLE GIVES TO SPIRITS

1. NAMES GIVEN TO DEMON SPIRITS IN THE NEW TESTAMENT

   There are many names in God's Word identifying evil spirits. Our Lord Jesus used a number of these Himself. Here is a list of references, from the New Testament.

   A. Blind spirit

   Matthew 12:22, *Then was brought unto him one possessed with a devil, blind, and dumb: and he healed him, insomuch that the blind and dumb both spake and saw.*

   B. Deaf and dumb spirit

   Mark 9:25, *When Jesus saw that the people came running together, he rebuked the foul spirit, saying unto him, Thou dumb and deaf spirit, I charge thee, come out of him, and enter no more into him.*

   C. "Unclean spirit" is used twenty-two times.

   Matthew 12:43, *When the unclean spirit is gone out of a man, he walketh through dry places, seeking rest, and findeth none.*

   Mark 1:23, *And there was in their synagogue a man with an unclean spirit; and he cried out.*

   Luke 9:42, *And as he was yet a-coming, the devil threw him down, and tare him. And Jesus rebuked the unclean spirit, and healed the child, and delivered him again to his father.*

     D.   Spirit of infirmity

Luke 13:11, *And, behold, there was a woman which had a spirit of infirmity eighteen years, and was bowed together, and could in no wise lift up herself.*

     E.   "Foul spirit" is used twenty-two times.

Mark 9:25, *When Jesus saw that the people came running together, he rebuked the foul spirit, saying unto him, Thou dumb and deaf spirit, I charge thee, come out of him, and enter no more into him.*

2.   OLD AND NEW TESTAMENT REFERENCES TO DEMON SPIRITS

There are other biblical references to demon spirits both in the Old and New Testaments.

     A.   Deluding and seducing spirits

I Timothy 4:1, *But the Holy Spirit distinctly and expressly declares that in latter times some will turn away from the faith, giving attention to deluding and seducing spirits and doctrines that demons teach. . .* (NKJV).

     B.   Angel of light

II Corinthians 11:14, *And no wonder! For Satan himself transforms himself into an angel of light* (NKJV).

     C.   "Jealous spirit" is used two times.

Numbers 5:29-31, *This is the law of jealousies, when a wife goeth aside to another instead of her husband, and is defiled;*
v. 30, *Or when the spirit of jealousy cometh upon him, and he be jealous over his wife, and shall set the woman before the LORD, and the priest shall execute upon her all this law.*
v. 31, *Then shall the man be guiltless from iniquity, and this woman shall bear her iniquity.*

     D.   Familiar spirit

Leviticus 20:6, 27, *And the person who turns after mediums and familiar spirits, to prostitute himself with them, I will set My face against that person and cut him off from his people.*

v. 27, *A man or a woman who is a medium, or who has familiar spirits, shall surely be put to death; they shall stone them with stones. Their blood shall be upon them* (NKJV).

> 2 Kings 23:24, *Moreover Josiah put away those who consulted mediums and spiritists, the household gods and idols, all the abominations that were seen in the land of Judah and in Jerusalem, that he might perform the words of the law which were written in the book that Hilkiah the priest found in the house of the LORD.*

3. DEMONS NAME THEMSELVES

In Mark 5:8-9 we have the account of Jesus' encounter with demons:

Mark 5:8-9, *For he said to him, Come out of the man, thou unclean spirit!*
v. 9, *And he asked him, What is thy name? And he answered, saying, My name is Legion: for we are many.*

4. DEMONS ARE LIARS

We must realize, however, that demons are liars and may not be telling the truth about their names, numbers, or strength. Evidently they vary in wickedness; some can be "more wicked" than others.

Matthew 12:45, *Then he goes and takes with him seven other spirits more wicked than himself, and they enter and dwell there; and the last state of that man is worse than the first. So shall it be with this wicked generation* (NKJV).

John 8:44, *You are of your father the devil, and the desires of your father you want to do. He was a murderer from the beginning, and does not stand in the truth, because there is no truth in him. When he speaks a lie, he speaks from his own resources, for he is a liar and the father of it* (NKJV).

5. DEMONS VARY IN POWER

Mark 9:17 & 28 relate the story of a boy possessed by a spirit that had robbed him of his speech. In verse 17, the disciples could not cast out the spirit. In verse 25, Jesus did. When the disciples asked Jesus about this, He said, *This kind cannot be driven out by anything but prayer and fasting.*

6. DEMONS HAVE WILLPOWER

Matthew 12:44, *Then he says, I will return to my house from which I came. And when he comes, he finds it empty, swept and put in order* (NKJV).

7. DEMONS VARY IN WICKEDNESS

Matthew 12:45, *Then goeth he, and taketh with himself seven other spirits more wicked than himself, and they enter in and dwell there: and the last state of that man is worse than the first. Even so shall it be also unto this wicked generation.*

8. DEMONS KNOW THE NAMES OF THOSE WHO REBUKE AND EXORCISE THEM

Acts 19:15, *And the evil spirit answered and said, Jesus I know, and Paul I know; but who are ye?*

Mark 1:24, *Saying, Let us alone; what have we to do with thee, thou Jesus of Nazareth? art thou come to destroy us? I know thee who thou art, the Holy One of God.*

9. DEMONS BELIEVE AND TREMBLE

Demons are not dead people any more than angels are glorified believers who have died and gone to heaven.

Demons believe in God, and, as James says, "they believe and tremble." Their belief is not one of faith, trust, and commitment; it is rather one of knowledge.

James 2:19, *Thou believest that there is one God; thou doest well: the devils also believe, and tremble.*

10. DEMONS ARE ORGANIZED

Ephesians 6:12, *For we wrestle not against flesh and blood, but against principalities, against powers, against the rulers of the darkness of this world, against spiritual wickedness in high places.*

11. DEMONS ARE SUBJECT TO CHRIST

The chief thing we all need to remember is that demons are subject to and under the sovereignty of the Lord Jesus Christ. Peter reminded the first-century believers of that when he wrote of Jesus in I Peter 3:22, *Who is gone into heaven, and is on the right hand of God; angels and authorities and powers being made subject unto him.*

12. DEMONS HAVE DOCTRINES

I Timothy 4:1, *Now the Spirit speaketh expressly, that in the latter times some shall depart from the faith, giving heed to seducing spirits, and doctrines of devils.*

13. TRUE DISCIPLES ARE GIVEN DIVINE AUTHORITY OVER DEMONS

We must all keep in mind that Jesus gave His disciples power and authority over all devils.

Luke 9:1, *Then he called his twelve disciples together, and gave them power and authority over all devils, and to cure diseases.*

Matthew 10:1, 8, *And when he had called unto him his twelve disciples, he gave them power against unclean spirits, to cast them out, and to heal all manner of sickness and all manner of disease.*

v. 8, *Heal the sick, cleanse the lepers, raise the dead, cast out devils: freely ye have received, freely give.*

II Timothy 1:7, *For God has not given us a spirit of fear, but of power and of love and of a sound mind.*

14.   WHAT DEMONS ARE NOT

Demons are not the spirits of dead people.

Demons are not the offspring of angels and men.

NOTES

_____
_____
_____
_____
_____
_____
_____
_____
_____
_____
_____
_____
_____
_____
_____
_____
_____
_____
_____
_____
_____
_____
_____
_____
_____
_____

STUDY GUIDE

INDIANA CHRISTIAN UNIVERSITY

DEMONOLOGY & DELIVERANCE I

Lesson 6

BIBLICAL NAMES FOR SATAN

INTRODUCTION:

Satan is the enigmatical personality of the universe. From his name you can identify his works. He is mentioned over two hundred times under many names. We will cover some of them in this chapter.

1. THE PRINCE OF THE AIR

    A.   In Ephesians 2:2 the devil is designated as, . . .*the prince of the power of the air.*

    "Prince" speaks of the exalted position of his rulership.

    "Power" speaks of the sphere of his rulership, which probably is the area above and around the earth.

    B.   Because Satan is a spirit, he can move through space with incredible speed, as other spirits can.

    Luke 10:18, *And he said unto them, I beheld Satan as lightning fall from heaven.*

    C.   It is significant that the designation *prince* is a name in the Bible given to deity, as to Jehovah.

    Daniel 8:11, *Yea, he magnified himself even to the prince of the host, and by him the daily sacrifice was taken away, and the place of his sanctuary was cast down.*

    1)   "Prince" is a designation given to Christ.

    Isaiah 9:6, *For unto us a child is born, unto us a son is given. . . The Prince of Peace.*

Acts 3:15, *And killed the Prince of life, whom God hath raised from the dead; whereof we are witnesses.*

Revelation 1:5, *And from Jesus Christ, who is the faithful witness, and the first begotten of the dead, and the prince of the kings of the earth...*

2) It is a name given to the chief priests of the temple.

Isaiah 43:28, *Therefore I have profaned the princes of the sanctuary, and have given Jacob to the curse, and Israel to reproaches.*

3) It is a name given to noblemen and kings.

Isaiah 10:8, *For he saith, Are not my princes altogether kings?*

Numbers 17:6, *And Moses spake unto the children of Israel, and every one of their princes gave him a rod apiece, for each prince one, according to their fathers' houses, even twelve rods: and the rod of Aaron was among their rods.*

4) This reveals the strength, power, and position the devil possesses through having been an archangel in heaven.

2. PRINCE OF THIS WORLD

Satan is sometimes described as the "prince of this world."

This means the unregenerated world; it means the world which has fallen from grace, the world that follows him to perdition.

John 12:31, *Now is the judgment of this world: now shall the prince of this world be cast out.*

John 16:11, *Of judgment, because the prince of this world is judged.*

3. PRINCE OF DARKNESS

A.   In Ephesians 6:12 Satan is described as the "prince of darkness." This reveals his black nature, and his complete disregard for light and holiness.

B.   All of his works are black and dark, for he is indeed the prince of all darkness.

C.   He is described as the prince of devils.

Matthew 12:24, *But when the Pharisees heard it, they said, This fellow doth not cast out devils, but by Beelzebub the prince of the devils.*

4. GOD OF THIS WORLD

A. He is called the god of this world.

II Corinthians 4:4, *In whom the god of this world hath blinded the minds of them which believe not, lest the light of the glorious gospel of Christ, who is the image of God, should shine unto them.*

B. Satan is the god of pagan people. They have strange manifestations in their worship of idols, but ultimately it is the devil they serve.

5. HE IS KING

A. Satan is a king over them of the bottomless pit.

Revelation 9:11, *And they had a king over them, which is the angel of the bottomless pit, whose name in the Hebrew tongue is Abaddon, but in the Greek tongue hath his name Apollyon.*

B. The devil has a kingdom.

Ephesians 6:12, *For we wrestle not against flesh and blood, but against principalities, against powers, against the rulers of the darkness of this world, against spiritual wickedness in high places.*

6. THE ANOINTED CHERUB

Ezekiel 28:14, *Thou art the anointed cherub that covereth; and I have set thee so: thou wast upon the holy mountain of God; thou hast walked up and down in the midst of the stones of fire.*

7. AN ANGEL OF LIGHT

The devil is called an angel of light. This has to do with his deception of mankind.

II Corinthians 11:14, *And no marvel; for Satan himself is transformed into an angel of light.*

He appeared to Eve in the Garden of Eden as a very kind and wonderful person. It was not until after she had sinned and fallen from God's grace that she discovered that the serpent had beguiled her.

Genesis 3:13, *And the LORD God said unto the woman, What is this that thou hast done? And the woman said, The serpent beguiled me, and I did eat.*

8. LUCIFER

Isaiah 14:12, *How art thou fallen from heaven, O Lucifer, son of the morning! how art thou cut down to the ground, which didst weaken the nations!*

9. DEVIL

    Revelation 12:9, *And the great dragon was cast out, that old serpent, called the Devil, and Satan, which deceiveth the whole world: he was cast out into the earth, and his angels were cast out with him.*

10. DRAGON

    Revelation 12:3, *And there appeared another wonder in heaven; and behold a great red dragon, having seven heads and ten horns, and seven crowns upon his heads.* (See Revelation 20:2-7 and Isaiah 14:29 for further reference.)

11. SATAN

    Job 1:6, *Now there was a day when the sons of God came to present themselves before the LORD, and Satan came also among them.*

12. SERPENT

    II Corinthians 11:3, *But I fear, lest by any means, as the serpent beguiled Eve through his subtilty, so your minds should be corrupted from the simplicity that is in Christ.* (See also Genesis 3:1, Revelation 12:9 and Genesis 3:14.)

13. BEELZEBUB

    A. Matthew 10:25, *It is enough for the disciple that he be as his master, and the servant as his lord. If they have called the master of the house Beelzebub, how much more shall they call them of his household?*

    B. Matthew 12:24, *But when the Pharisees heard it, they said, This fellow doth not cast out devils, but by Beelzebub the prince of the devils.*

14. BELIAL

    II Corinthians 6:15, *And what concord hath Christ with Belial? or what part hath he that believeth with an infidel?*

15. ADVERSARY

    I Peter 5:8, *Be sober, be vigilant; because your adversary the devil, as a roaring lion, walketh about, seeking whom he may devour.*

16. **ACCUSER OF THE BRETHREN**

   A. Revelation 12:10, *And I heard a loud voice saying in heaven, Now is come salvation, and strength, and the kingdom of our God, and the power of his Christ: for the accuser of our brethren is cast down, which accused them before our God day and night.*

   B. Job 1:7-8, *And the LORD said unto Satan, Whence comest thou? Then Satan answered the LORD, and said, From going to and fro in the earth, and from walking up and down in it.*
   v. 8, And the LORD said unto Satan, Hast thou considered my servant Job, that there is none like him in the earth, a perfect and an upright man, one that feareth God, and escheweth evil?

17. **THE ENEMY**

   Matthew 13:39, *The enemy that sowed them is the devil; the harvest is the end of the world; and the reapers are the angels.*

18. **THE TEMPTER**

   Matthew 4:3, *And when the tempter came to him, he said, If thou be the Son of God, command that these stones be made bread.*

19. **THE WICKED ONE**

   Matthew 13:19, *When any one heareth the word of the kingdom, and understandeth it not, then cometh the wicked one, and catcheth away that which was sown in his heart. This is he which received seed by the way side.*

20. **THE THIEF**

   John 10:10, *The thief cometh not, but for to steal, and to kill, and to destroy: I am come that they might have life, and that they might have it more abundantly.*

21. **MURDERER**

   John 8:44a, *Ye are of your father the devil, and the lusts of your father ye will do. He was a murderer from the beginning, . . .*

22. **A ROARING LION**

   I Peter 5:8, *Be sober, be vigilant; because your adversary the devil, as a roaring lion, walketh about, seeking whom he may devour.*

31

23. A LIAR

John 8:44, *Ye are of your father the devil, . . .there is no truth in him. When he speaketh a lie, he speaketh of his own: for he is a liar, and the father of it.*

24. AN OPPRESSOR

Peter is speaking here in Acts 10:23-48, explaining to a large gathering all that had taken place.

Acts 10:38, *How God anointed Jesus of Nazareth with the Holy Ghost and with power: who went about doing good, and healing all that were oppressed of the devil; for God was with him.*

25. THE CORRUPTER OF MINDS

II Corinthians 11:3, *But I fear, lest by any means, as the serpent beguiled Eve through his subtilty, so your minds should be corrupted from the simplicity that is in Christ.*

26. ABADDON--APOLLYON

Revelation 9:11, *And they had a king over them, which is the angel of the bottomless pit, whose name in the Hebrew tongue is Abaddon, but in the Greek tongue hath his name Apollyon.*

DEMONOLOGY & DELIVERANCE I

Lesson 7

WHERE TO RECOGNIZE DEMON POWER PART I

INTRODUCTION:

Thinking people today are rapidly coming to realize that there are definite, invisible spiritual forces arrayed in battle against humanity. These forces are not discernible in just one avenue of modern life, but many.

Strange happenings indicate that a power that is other than human is struggling to dominate the modern world.

A restlessness exists within society that defies explanation. It all points to the supernatural activities of demon power.

The irony and tragedy of it all is that the less the church teaches about demon power, the more control the devil takes over society. Most of the world is possessed by the devil and his demonic forces, and the rest of the world does not believe the devil exists, and the devil sees to it that the two never meet.

The church needs to say with the Apostle Paul in II Corinthians 2:11, . . .*we are not ignorant of his devices.* The church needs to carry out the Great Commission of Christ in full--not just to preach the good news to the ends of the earth, but to cast out devils by the power of Christ.

READING:

Mark 16:15-18, *And he said unto them, Go ye into all the world, and preach the gospel to every creature.*
v. 16, *He that believeth and is baptized shall be saved; but he that believeth not shall be damned.*
v. 17, *And these signs shall follow them that believe; In my name shall they cast out devils; they shall speak with new tongues;*

v. 18, *They shall take up serpents; and if they drink any deadly thing, it shall not hurt them; they shall lay hands on the sick, and they shall recover.*

1. **SEVEN AREAS OF MODERN LIFE WHERE DEMON POWER CAN BE RECOGNIZED**

    1)   World of apostate religion

    2)   World of business

    3)   World of politics

    4)   World of crime

    5)   World of occultism

    6)   World of disease

    7)   World of morals

2. **WORLD OF APOSTATE RELIGION AND DEMON POWER**

    I Timothy 4:1, *Now the Spirit speaketh expressly, that in the latter times some shall depart from the faith, giving heed to seducing spirits, and doctrines of devils.*

    A.   Bible-believing Christians today are persuaded that we are living in the final crisis of this dispensation. They believe that it is the greatest crisis of the last 2,000 years.

    B.   We believe that we shall see amazing phenomena of angels and demons. Christians will find angels supporting and succoring them. Already there are reports of the manifestations of angels in various places.

    C.   There will be more demon activity, more people possessed and oppressed, than the world has ever known.

    D.   The church must rise to the occasion and command the power of Jesus Christ to set men and women free.

    E.   Without the power of God, the church will fail in its last duty to mankind before the Lord returns for His bride.

    F.   The Apostle Paul warns in I Timothy 4:1, *Now the Spirit speaketh expressly, that in the latter times some shall depart from the faith, giving heed to seducing spirits, and doctrines of devils.*

    A seducing spirit is a lying a spirit, a deceiving spirit. "Doctrines of devils" means exactly what it says.

1) Satan has always had doctrines which he proclaims.

2) He told Eve that she would not die if she disobeyed God.

3) He asked Christ to become selfish and make bread for Himself, and finally to worship him.

4) Doctrines of devils will take whoever believes them to hell.

3. IS THIS PROPHECY BEING FULFILLED TODAY?

I believe that it is. Cults, spiritism, and all groups who have their own book to lead them, as well as Christian Scientists, Jehovah's Witnesses, Mormons, etc., who have added their doctrines to the Bible, are part of the apostasy of the last days. When Satan leads anyone into error, he leads him from error to error. There is no terminus. There is a vast revival of Satanism and witchcraft that are forms of devil worship.

I Corinthians 10:20, *But I say, that the things which the Gentiles sacrifice, they sacrifice to devils, and not to God: and I would not that ye should have fellowship with devils.*

NOTES

_____

_____

_____

_____

_____

_____

_____

_____

_____

_____

_____

_____

_____

_____

_____

_____

_____

_____

_____

_____

_____

_____

_____

_____

_____

STUDY GUIDE

INDIANA CHRISTIAN UNIVERSITY

DEMONOLOGY & DELIVERANCE I

Lesson 8

WHERE TO RECOGNIZE DEMON POWER PART II

READING:

James 5:1-6, *Go to now, ye rich men, weep and howl for your miseries that shall come upon you.*
v. 2, *Your riches are corrupted, and your garments are motheaten.*
v. 3, *Your gold and silver is cankered; and the rust of them shall be a witness against you, and shall eat your flesh as it were fire. Ye have heaped treasure together for the last days.*
v. 4, *Behold, the hire of the labourers who have reaped down your fields, which is of you kept back by fraud, crieth: and the cries of them which have reaped are entered into the ears of the Lord of sabaoth.*
v. 5, *Ye have lived in pleasure on the earth, and been wanton; ye have nourished your hearts, as in a day of slaughter.*
v. 6, *Ye have condemned and killed the just; and he doth not resist you.*

1. WORLD OF BUSINESS AND DEMON POWER

    A.   New Testament writers warn against the evil of covetousness and greed. The Apostle Paul equates it with idolatry.

           Colossians 3:5, *So kill (deaden, deprive of power) the evil desire lurking in your members—those animal impulses and all that is earthly in you that is employed in sin: sexual vice, impurity, sensual appetites, unholy desires, and all greed and covetousness, for that in idolatry [the defying of self and other created things instead of God]* (AMP).

B. The love and lust for money is a spirit and another area in which we may expect increased demon power in the days ahead.

I John 2:15-17, *Love not the world, neither the things that are in the world. If any man love the world, the love of the Father is not in him.*
v. 16, *For all that is in the world, the lust of the flesh, and the lust of the eyes, and the pride of life, is not of the Father, but is of the world.*
v. 17, *And the world passeth away, and the lust thereof: but he that doeth the will of God abideth for ever.*

C. The Bible says that the love of money is the root of all evil.

I Timothy 6:10, *For the love of money is the root of all evil: which while some coveted after, they have erred from the faith, and pierced themselves through with many sorrows.*

D. Many people lust after and are addicted to money and the things money can buy.

I Timothy 6:9, *But those who crave to be rich fall into temptation and a snare, and into many foolish (useless, godless) and hurtful desires that plunge men into ruin and destruction and miserable perishing* (AMP).

Greed is as much a narcotic to them as heroin is to the dope addict.

Hebrews 13:5, *Let your conduct be without covetousness, and be content with such things as you have. For He Himself has said, "I will never leave you nor forsake you"* (NKJV).

Because of covetousness and greed:

1) People abuse their families. They cheat and lie.

2) They sell their reputations as well as their bodies and souls.

3) Almost every evil in the world can be traced to the love or lust of money.

 Mark 7:21-23, *For from within, out of the heart of men, proceed evil thoughts, adulteries, fornications, murders,*
 v. 22, *Thefts, covetousness, wickedness, deceit, lasciviousness, an evil eye, blasphemy, pride, foolishness.*
 v. 23, *All these evil things come from within, and defile the man.*

4) Homes are broken into, and men rob and kill.

5) We read in newspapers about the death from malnutrition of an old recluse whose mattress and secret hiding places yielded more than $100,000.

Many Americans today have allowed the dollar to become their master.

That is of the devil. Covetousness will increase in these last days.

God wants us to love Him and not the things of the world. The devil will rule big business in the future.

Jesus said, *Take heed and beware of covetousness, for one's life does not consist in the abundance of the things he possesses* (Luke 12:15 NKJV).

2. WORLD OF POLITICS AND DEMON POWER

A. Satanic opposition in the biblical political world of the past is seen in the experience of Daniel. Daniel prayed and fasted for his people but did not get an answer. After twenty-one days, an angel of God came to him and said:

Daniel 10:12-13, *. . .Fear not, Daniel: for from the first day that thou didst set thine heart to understand, and to chasten thyself before thy God, thy words were heard, and I am come for thy words.*
v. 13, *But the prince of the kingdom of Persia withstood me one and twenty days: but, lo, Michael, one of the chief princes, came to help me; and I remained there with the kings of Persia.*

This incident affords a tremendous revelation of the unseen battles being fought in the spirit, in the realm of governments and nations.

B. The incident of Herod's destroying the children of Bethlehem is another instance.

Matthew 2:16-18, *Then Herod, when he saw that he was mocked of the wise men, was exceeding wroth, and sent forth, and slew all the children that were in Bethlehem, and in all the coasts thereof, from two years old and under, according to the time which he had diligently inquired of the wise men.*
v. 17, *Then was fulfilled that which was spoken by Jeremy the prophet, saying,*
v. 18, *In Rama was there a voice heard, lamentation, and weeping, and great mourning, Rachel weeping for her children, and would not be comforted, because they are not.*

Herod was controlled by demonic power.

3. WORLD OF CRIME AND DEMON POWER

A. Modern crime is evidently related to demon power. Isaiah the prophet described the working of crime: these are conditions which are true of the day and age in which we live.

Isaiah 59:3-4, *For your hands are defiled with blood, and your fingers with iniquity; your lips have spoken lies, your tongue hath muttered perverseness.*

v. 4, *None calleth for justice, nor any pleadeth for truth: they trust in vanity, and speak lies; they conceive mischief, and bring forth iniquity.*

B. Demon power is a driving force. Jesus declared that in the last days iniquity shall abound.

Matthew 24:12, *And because iniquity shall abound, the love of many shall wax cold.*

He was speaking in terms broader than man's inhumanity to man. He was encompassing the last assault of Satan upon the human family. Knowing that his time is short, Satan has unleashed his demon forces to do violence and to take peace from the earth. Crimes are committed under strange delusions and compulsions. For example:

1) A mother strangled her little child to death. "A voice told me to do it," she confessed to police afterward.

2) In another city a man cut up a human body, put it in a suitcase and carried it around with him. He is not crazy, for he knows how to drive a car and do his work.

3) A husband shot his wife and family and told police that a spirit told him to do this.

Examples like this are to be found in almost every daily newspaper around the world.

C. The compulsion to kill has to come from deep inner drives that can only be explained as diabolical. Demon power is seen not only as the driving force behind the brutal nature of modern crime, but also behind the more subtle, pervasive "spirit of the age" which motivates people to do evil. How can we counteract the "spirit of the age?" How can we break the hold of demons over men?

1) Christ possesses greater power than that of devils.

I John 4:4, *. . . greater is he that is in you, than he that is in the world.*

2) Jesus can break demonic power over men.

Matthew 12:28, *But if I cast out devils by the Spirit of God, then the kingdom of God is come unto you.*

He was making it possible for them to observe His power over demonic forces.

3) Our Lord gave authority over devils to His disciples.

Mark 16:17, *And these signs shall follow them that believe; In my name shall they cast out devils; they shall speak with new tongues.*

Luke 10:17, *And the seventy returned again with joy, saying, Lord, even the devils are subject unto us through thy name.*

4) A Christian must have power to bind the strong man, the devil. Then he can spoil his goods and set the devil's victim free.

Matthew 12:29, *Or else how can one enter into a strong man's house, and spoil his goods, except he first bind the strong man? and then he will spoil his house.*

4. OCCULTISM AND DEMON POWER

A. For many years, America has sent missionaries to foreign lands to deliver those who were demon possessed. They brought life and hope through the gospel and set them free. Today heathen religions are invading this country in an unprecedented way. Large cities in America have become centers of false cults and demon worship.

Eternity Magazine states there are over 2,000 witches in the greater Philadelphia area alone. Witchcraft is a growing movement among today's New Agers who claim that it is a legitimate religion which has strong similarities to Eastern religions.

The Bible warns us to avoid the dangers of practicing witchcraft and occultism.

Deuteronomy 18:10-12, *There shall not be found among you any one. . .that useth divination, or an observer of times, or an enchanter, or a witch, or a charmer, or a consulter with familiar spirits, or a wizard, or a necromancer. For all that do these are an abomination to the LORD. . .* (See also Galatians 5:20 and Revelation 9:20-21).

Heathen religions are growing in the big cities. Many of these religions propagate the doctrine of reincarnation. The unbiblical concepts of karma and reincarnation are almost universally accepted by New Agers.

Paul warned young Timothy of the doctrines of devils that he was certain to encounter. The warning is for us today:

I Timothy 6:20, *O Timothy, keep that which is committed to thy trust, avoiding profane and vain babblings, and oppositions of science falsely so called:*

The Bible makes it clear that demon activity will be as prevalent, if not more so, at the end of this age as it was in the days of our Lord. It is significant that all specific demon activity referred to after the ascension of Christ is in relation to the end of this age. We have been warned that demon activity will be prevalent and powerful and violent.

Jude vv. 17-21, *But, beloved, remember ye the words which were spoken before of the apostles of our Lord Jesus Christ;*
v. 18, *How that they told you there should be mockers in the last time, who should walk after their own ungodly lusts.*
v. 19, *These be they who separate themselves, sensual, having not the Spirit.*
v. 20, *But ye, beloved, building up yourselves on your most holy faith, praying in the Holy Ghost,*
v. 21, *Keep yourselves in the love of God, looking for the mercy of our Lord Jesus Christ unto eternal life.*

B. In the closing days of the age, demons set the stage for Antichrist. The chief "props" used in this grand deception are religion and demon worship.

Mark 13:22, *. . .false Christs and false prophets shall rise, and shall shew signs and wonders, to seduce, if it were possible, even the elect.*

C. Persistent rejection of truth destroys one's sense of truth and lays a person open to being deceived by unrighteousness and to the works of Satan with all power and signs and lying wonders.

2 Thessalonians 2:7-12, *For the mystery of iniquity doth already work: only he who now letteth will let, until he be taken out of the way.*
v. 8, *And then shall that Wicked be revealed, whom the Lord shall consume with the spirit of his mouth, and shall destroy with the brightness of his coming:* (Isaiah 11:4)
v. 9, *Even him, whose coming is after the working of Satan with all power and signs and lying wonders,*
v. 10, *And with all deceivableness of unrighteousness in them that perish; because they received not the love of the truth, that they might be saved.*
v. 11, *And for this cause God shall send them strong delusion, that they should believe a lie:*
v. 12, *That they all might be damned who believed not the truth, but had pleasure in unrighteousness.*

D. An empty and confused soul becomes a sign to the devil, "House to let."

E.   The devil and his demons take up a vacancy. This explains why we are seeing such widespread activity of demons in religion and worship. As the soul of man becomes increasingly depleted spiritually, his soul becomes an unguarded fortress into which demon powers have open access.

Luke 11:24-26, *When the unclean spirit is gone out of a man, he walketh through the dry places, seeking rest; and finding none, he saith, I will return unto my house whence I came out.*
v. 25, *And when he cometh, he findeth it swept and garnished.*
v. 26, *Then goeth he, and taketh to him seven other spirits more wicked than himself; and they enter in, and dwell there: and the last state of that man is worse than the first.*

Men whose souls are empty and hungry will feed upon anything that promises satisfaction, even if it is poisoned.

F.   According to the New Testament, a great outburst of demon activity is to be expected at the end of this age. Satan's master plan is to undermine the faith of believers and to destroy the church from within.

1)   It will manifest itself in movements that will deceive people in doctrinal and ethical matters and will culminate in the possessing and guiding of the kings of this earth by the demons themselves. This happened already in the early days of the church. Acts 15:24 speaks of those who sought to "subvert souls," disturbing and unsettling people's minds with their teachings, "throwing them into confusion." It is happening today.

2)   We have seen certain characters in history, anarchists and Christ-haters, who are demon possessed. They give us an illustration of what to expect at the end of this age.

2 Thessalonians 2:3-4 teaches of the great apostasy, the falling away of every Christian church and Jewish temple in the world. Texe Marr in his book, *Dark Secrets of the New Age*, explains what is believed to be the plan of the "New Age World Religion":

"New Age leaders are convinced that they will vanquish and destroy the Christian churches of America and the West without so much as a whisper of protest from the tens of millions of Christians in those churches. What's more, they believe that their takeover of Christianity will be welcomed by most Christian ministers and laymen. Their victory, these New Age leaders say, will come as Christians abandon their current outmoded doctrines en masse and enthusiastically adopt those of the New Age!"

The orthodox Jewish faith is also a target, with its belief in God Almighty and the primacy of the Old Testament.

The New Age truly believes that its current campaign of subtle subversion and quiet undermining of Christian doctrine will result in total victory. It will not be necessary to stage a direct, frontal assault on Christianity. What is planned is an insidious, veiled attack. The horrible intent of the leaders of the New Age is to invade and conquer Christianity much as bacteria do a living organism. The end result will be to leave the Christian body a rotting corpse, full of worms and eaten away from within."

Marr quotes William Thompson, avid New Age writer and intellectual who wrote: "The new spirituality does not reject the earlier patterns of the great universal religions. Priest and church will not disappear; they will not be forced out of existence in the New Age, they will be absorbed into the existence of the New Age."

Marr concludes: "Dictators learned long ago that willing acceptance by a people is far preferable to forced repression. To threaten Christianity with open destruction is not Satan's style. He knows that it only invites counterattacks, and he does not wish to awaken and alarm those who might oppose him. Satan plays the game dirty, with trickery and treachery. He makes inside moves. His is the tactic of the Trojan horse."

3) We have briefly considered some of the factors spread in the world today, which will make possible this outburst of demon possession.

a) The empty soul of modern man devoid of faith in God

b) The increase of spiritism

c) The widespread increase of immorality which can be linked with the uncleanness of these evil spirits

d) The growing significance of what is called thought control

Bible-believing Christians agree that our generation is yielding itself to demon influences in an unprecedented manner.

5. WORLD OF DISEASE AND DEMON POWER

A startling truth is that our modern world has more hospitals than at any previous period of history. There are more doctors ready to serve. Science has produced more medicine of every description, yet our world has more sickness than man has ever known. This must be a demonic situation.

Satan is an inhuman, merciless fiend whose ultimate goal is the destruction of the human race. He is a devourer (1 Peter 5:8). The book of Revelation speaks of the seven last plagues (Revelation 21:9) and that the earth would be struck with plagues (Revelation 11:6). It speaks of the pains and the loathsome and malignant sores (Revelation 16:2, 11).

6. WORLD OF MORALS

A. We have observed an amazing increase in demonic power and satanic activity in the degeneration of morals. We are approaching a time when the entire community will be under fierce attack by immoral spirits.

B. Family life in America will continue to fall apart.

C. Men and women will live on an animal level, changing homes promiscuously. It is possible that adultery is a spirit.

D. Any attempt to curb obscenity is thwarted by powerful forces which have both money and the opinion makers on their side. The real untouchables in this country, says one newspaper columnist, are the writers, publishers, and salesmen of smut. They are prospering financially. The money and the lobby for smut are powerful. Opposition to obscenity is regarded as a witch hunt.

E. Moral perversion will increase in a most dreadful and horrible way. I believe sodomy to be a spirit. This sin is causing consternation throughout the world and is putrefying society. One can see why God would destroy great cities like Sodom and Gomorrah, yet today literature glorifying sexual perversion is sold on practically every newsstand in the country.

To communicate one's own sick pathology, especially if one is a pervert, is now regarded as the highest art form and the quickest entry into the genius sweepstakes. Recent court rulings all over the country, from the lowest to the highest courts, have decreed that anything goes. The Lord Jesus Christ said in Luke 17:28, 30, . . .*as it was in the days of Lot. . . Even thus shall it be in the day when the Son of man is revealed.*

God hates sodomy no less today than he did in Lot's day when He brought awful judgment. Anyone who indulges in it is possessed and needs divine deliverance. Psychiatry cannot deliver from perversions; only the power of Christ can set men and women free.

The modern church must be able to meet the needs of the people, otherwise the church has no good reason to exist.

God is able and willing to set anyone free from an immoral spirit.

The powerful words of 1 John 4 caution us to test the spirits so that we can recognize the Spirit of God. (Read this chapter and let its truths penetrate your thinking.) The apostle concludes with these words found in chapter 5:

1 John 5:20-21, *And we know that the Son of God is come, and hath given us an understanding, that we may know him that is true, and we are in him that is true, even in his Son Jesus Christ. This is the true God, and eternal life.*
v. 21, *Little children, keep yourselves from idols. Amen.*

STUDY GUIDE

INDIANA CHRISTIAN UNIVERSITY

DEMONOLOGY & DELIVERANCE I

Lesson 9

AREAS OF DEMON DOMINATION PART I

INTRODUCTION:

It is an historical fact that the devil's influence can dominate and even destroy empires and nations.

READING:

Revelation 18:2, . . . *Babylon the great is fallen, is fallen, and is become the habitation of devils, and the hold of every foul spirit. . .*

1. THE BIBLE ESTABLISHES THIS TRUTH

God, speaking through His prophet Isaiah, related the fall of Lucifer with these words:

Isaiah 14:12-17, *How art thou fallen from heaven, O Lucifer, son of the morning! how art thou cut down to the ground, which didst weaken the nations!*
v. 13, *For thou hast said in thine heart, I will ascend into heaven, I will exalt my throne above the stars of God: I will sit also upon the mount of the congregation, in the sides of the north:*
v. 14, *I will ascend above the heights of the clouds: I will be like the most High.*
v. 15, *Yet thou shalt be brought down to hell, to the sides of the pit.*
v. 16, *They that see thee shall narrowly look upon thee, and consider thee, saying, Is this the man that made the earth to tremble, that did shake kingdoms;*
v. 17, *That made the world as a wilderness, and destroyed the cities thereof; that opened not the house of his prisoners?*

47

2. HOW CAN SATAN MAKE THE EARTH TREMBLE?

A. An example of this is Napoleon the Great. The devil caused him to bring war upon the continent of Europe. Through Napoleon's destroying Europe with his bloodthirsty armies, God saw Lucifer energizing and inspiring Napoleon to make the earth tremble.

B. This is also true of men like Alexander the Great. Humans recorded his natural victories. God saw the driving force that made him desire to kill and destroy to exalt himself. The fact that Alexander was under demon power is also revealed in the way he died in a drunken orgy at the age of thirty-three.

C. In more modern times, we saw the same influence in men like Hitler and Mussolini who made boastful statements of how they would dominate the world. It is said of Mussolini that he declared, "I would shake hands with the devil if he would help me get the desire of my heart."

D. God truly said of Lucifer that he was the one who made the world a wilderness. The Bible clearly states that Babylon was controlled by unseen powers of evil and was finally judged.

Isaiah 13:19-20, *And Babylon, the glory of kingdoms, the beauty of the Chaldees' excellency, shall be as when God overthrew Sodom and Gomorrah.* v. 20, *It shall never be inhabited, neither shall it be dwelt in from generation to generation. . .*

We understand that much of the world's witchcraft was born in Babylon. It was cultivated and distributed from there to destroy the whole world by the worship of Lucifer.

3. ANCIENT NATIONS AND DEVILS

Unseen demon powers dominated nations in the past. History records the sinister works of evil.

A. It is remarkable how the people of Israel fought the devil's power as a nation.

Exodus 22:18, *Thou shalt not suffer a witch to live.*

God knew that these people would turn the entire nation over to the devil.

B. God removed Saul from his kingship, and he died for his transgression of seeking after witchcraft.

1 Chronicles 10:13, *So Saul died for his transgression which he committed against the LORD, even against the word of the LORD, which he kept not, and also for asking counsel of one that had a familiar spirit, to inquire of it.*

God would not permit His land and people to be taken over by demon power.

4. MODERN NATIONS AND DEVILS

A. I have visited countries which make me feel very sad and depressed. One such country is Indonesia. I preached through that country from one end to the other for a number of months, and I am sincere when I say I have never seen so much demon power as there is in Indonesia. I have never seen so many witch doctors in any other country.

B. While ministering in Singapore, I found that heathen worshipers must pay respect to Pa, a powerful dignitary who is the spiritual ruler of the area, before they can worship other gods. The heathen worshipers go to his temple and pray before daring to worship in other places. This is practiced today.

C. All heathen countries are under the power of Satan. There are different categories of spirits, possessing varying degrees of power and authority.

D. There are lands like Tibet, where the devil has held supremacy for ages. I have personally traveled into Tibetan country among the high mountains of Southwest China. I slept in their heathen temples (there was no other place to sleep), saw the idol-filled temples, and listened to strange stories of demon power.

5. NATIONS OF THE FUTURE WILL WORSHIP THE DEVIL

During the period of the great tribulation on this earth, as described in Revelation, we see that the dragon, Satan, will be worshiped.

Revelation 13:4, *And they worshipped the dragon which gave power unto the beast: and they worshipped the beast, saying, Who is like unto the beast? who is able to make war with him?*

6. CITIES AND DEVILS

A. Not only does the devil seek to rule empires and nations, he seeks to dominate cities. One of the churches of the Apocalypse was located in Pergamos, a great and historic city. Pergamos was beautiful, but the Bible says that it was one of the cities where Satan's seat was located.

Revelation 2:12-13, *And to the angel of the church in Pergamos write; These things saith he which hath the sharp sword with two edges;*
v. 13, *I know thy works, and where thou dwellest, even where Satan's seat is: and thou holdest fast my name, and hast not denied my faith, even in those days wherein Antipas was my faithful martyr, who was slain among you, where Satan dwelleth.*

This indicates that there are cities where devils set up their thrones and rule. The devil's power is centralized in such places. In these cities Satan has greater strength than he has elsewhere to perform his horrible deeds. There are two areas mentioned here: where "Satan dwelleth" and "Satan's seat." This speaks of the headquarters from which Satan operates, and of a throne from which he dictates to his evil spirits the work they are to do.

B. History vividly points out such cities. For example, ancient Babylon gave itself over to sorceries, witchcraft, and cults. Without a doubt, that queen city, which boasted of its hanging gardens, was also dominated by an evil spirit which kept Daniel's prayer from being answered when he lived in Babylon.

Daniel 10:20-21, *Then said he, Knowest thou wherefore I come unto thee? and now will I return to fight with the prince of Persia: and when I am gone forth, lo, the prince of Grecia shall come.*
v. 21, *But I will shew thee that which is noted in the scripture of truth: and there is none that holdeth with me in these things, but Michael your prince.*

The angel said that when he left Daniel, he would have to fight a spirit called the prince of Persia, and that only Michael was available to assist him in his warfare. This reveals that evidently there are cosmic battles that take place over big cities.

C. The cities of Sodom and Gomorrah are remarkable examples of demon habitation. These cities gave themselves to a very peculiar and terrible sin, which bears the name of the cities until this day. The spirit that ruled there caused men to make love with men rather than with women. Only the devil could have caused this to happen. Sodomy became so dominant that God was obligated to wipe that sinful city off the face of the earth. Sodom was a city where Satan's seat was and where Satan dwelled. Here the devil commanded supreme power.

D. The devil has not changed. There are modern cities which have given themselves to certain sins which only an evil spirit could bring. I am sure you are aware of the fact that every city has a spirit in it and that no two cities in the world possess the same spirit. I am very sensitive to the presence of the spirit that rules in a city. Naturally, some cities have a good spirit; others have a bad spirit. No doubt you have heard different ministers say that while a certain city is very hard and very difficult to work in, another seems to be open to the movement and the Spirit of God.

I am sure that a big metropolis like New York City is possessed of a special kind of spirit. The majority of the population do not attend church. Many of the people there live in the deepest sin. New York is a center of commerce for the world, and a center for world government. If one's spiritual eyes could be opened, no doubt he would be able to see that strong and evil spirits rule there.

NOTES

_____

_____

_____

_____

_____

_____

_____

_____

_____

_____

_____

_____

_____

_____

_____

_____

_____

_____

_____

_____

_____

_____

_____

STUDY GUIDE

INDIANA CHRISTIAN UNIVERSITY

DEMONOLOGY & DELIVERANCE I

Lesson 10

AREAS OF DEMON DOMINATION PART II

1. BIG CITIES OF AMERICA

I feel sure that a city like Hollywood, California, is dominated by an evil spirit. It is a spirit of immorality--a sensual, lustful spirit. In the past, several young couples I knew personally moved from our part of the country into the Hollywood area. Before long, they were divorced, and some of them were remarried. If they had stayed in the part of the country from which they came, this thing likely would never have happened. Living in an area where Satan is strong in destroying morals, they fell beneath his onslaught.

It seems that the big cities of America are becoming increasingly difficult to reach for God. I believe that the devil's power is taking a stranglehold upon them. I have observed that many Full Gospel churches are even smaller than they were several years ago. If there was ever a time when the gospel power should invade big cities to bind the devil and set the people free, it is today.

Big cities dominate our country. Much of the filth on television comes from two great centers--Hollywood and New York. Most of the amusement that is wicked and immoral comes from big cities. They dominate whole areas. I am sure we need to attack these cities spiritually and defeat the devil.

I humbly feel that if I had not prayed for a girl in Bilibid Prison in Manila, Philippines, and wrestled for two days with the evil spirit which possessed her, the great revival would not have come to the city of Manila. I believe that we should not give the great cities of this world to the devil!

2.   CALCUTTA, INDIA

I found the city of Calcutta, India, to be one of the most depressing cities on the face of the earth. The city is named after a female goddess named Cali. Cali is a fierce devil. When you see her image at the great temple, her tongue sticks out about six inches wide and eight inches long. This goddess demands blood. Her followers must bring goats to the temple and cut their throats, letting the blood flow in a groove underneath this hideous idol. Her devotees splash their faces and drink the hot goat blood. The Cali Temple in Calcutta is also a place of gross immorality, for it is claimed that this goddess can give children to barren women. I saw a tree full of horrible looking heathen artifacts tied to the branches. The devotees came and tied them to the tree and prayed to the goddess Cali. Often, people deeply under her influence are subject to violent fits. To win Calcutta to Christ, one certainly will have to face that devil in combat.

One of our missionaries told me that he prayed for a person a hundred miles away from Calcutta and found her to be demon possessed. The missionary said, "Who are you?" The evil spirit spoke through the person and said, "I am from Cali in Calcutta." Then the missionary said, "Come out of her in Jesus' name." The devil came out crying and weeping, saying, "Now I must journey back to Calcutta to find somebody else in which to live."

I have spoken to several people who have spiritual discernment. Invariably they say that the city of Calcutta is shackled with a spirit of oppression. Without doubt, such cities have wicked dignitaries dominating them in the world of the spirit.

3.   INDONESIA

While traveling in Indonesia, we found what the people call "Cities of Devils." These are cities where the chief priests of demon worship, black magic, and spiritism have their headquarters. The doctors of witchcraft congregate in these cities and work out from them. Beyond any doubt these cities have spiritual darkness much greater than other cities in Indonesia.

4.   JESUS' BIG CITY: JERUSALEM

It is interesting to me that Jesus wept over Jerusalem. It was the big city of His life.

Today we should weep over the great cities of our land lest they become throne rooms of the devil's power. The reason the evil one's power is stronger in the big cities like Washington, New York, Chicago, and Los Angeles is because they are full of soothsayers, crystal-gazers, fortune tellers, spiritist mediums, and cults of all kinds.

But there is no power that can stand before the living Church. The Lord Jesus promised that even the gates of hell could not stop His Church. Let's advance on the big cities.

DEMONOLOGY & DELIVERANCE I

Lesson 11

AREAS OF DEMON DOMINATION PART III

1. HUMANS, ANIMALS, AND DEMONS

   Luke 8:30, *And Jesus asked him, saying, What is thy name? And he said, Legion: because many devils were entered into him.*

   A. There are three areas spoken of in God's Word regarding demons in individuals and animals.

      1) Beasts may be possessed by devils. The story of some pigs into which devils entered and how they plunged down a steep slope into the sea, perishing in the water, is told in Matthew 8:29-32, *And, behold, they cried out, saying, What have we to do with thee, Jesus, thou Son of God? art thou come hither to torment us before the time?*
      v. 30, *And there was a good way off from them an herd of many swine feeding.*
      v. 31, *So the devils besought him, saying, If thou cast us out, suffer us to go away into the herd of swine.*
      v. 32, *And he said unto them, Go. And when they were come out, they went into the herd of swine: and, behold, the whole herd of swine ran violently down a steep place into the sea, and perished in the waters.*

      I am sure farmers and other people who deal with animals have noticed peculiar beasts which actually possessed a strange spirit, and possibly had to be destroyed because they could not live peaceably with other animals or with humans.

      2) Parts of a human body can be possessed. Several times Jesus cast out spirits of deafness and dumbness from human beings.

Matthew 9:32, *As they went out, behold, they brought to him a dumb man possessed with a devil.*

He also cast out the spirit of infirmity from a person. This means that an evil spirit can take over a certain part of the human body and not remove itself until someone with God's power rebukes it with divine authority (see Luke 8:2).

3) Unregenerate mankind can come under the complete domination and authority of the devil. Jesus tells about a man who was demon possessed, blind and mute. When delivered of that evil spirit, he both spoke and saw. The spirit walked through dry places looking for a place of rest, but could not find one. Sometime later, this same spirit returned to look upon the man. He found his soul swept and garnished, but empty.

Matthew 12:43-44, *When the unclean spirit is gone out of a man, he walketh through dry places, seeking rest, and findeth none.*
v. 44, *Then he saith, I will return into my house from whence I came out; and when he is come, he findeth it empty, swept, and garnished.*

Being swept means that the world had been taken away from him; garnished means decorated. The man's religious decorations were all right. He looked religious, he may have carried hymnals and prayer books. But his spirit was empty. The demon instantly realized that this man had no resistance to him. Therefore, he went back into the dry places and found seven other evil spirits even worse than himself. Together they came back, overwhelmed this man and possessed him. Jesus said that the last end of that man was worse than the first. This story about devils going in and out of a human being was told by the Lord Jesus Christ Himself.

B. Jesus came to this world to deliver men from the devil's power.

Acts 10:38, *. . .God anointed Jesus of Nazareth with the Holy Ghost and with power: who went about doing good, and healing all that were oppressed of the devil; for God was with him.*

1) In Luke 8:2 we read of certain women who were healed of evil spirits and infirmities, and of Mary Magdalene, who was delivered of seven devils.

Here is one of the most remarkable of Bible events. The Bible says specifically and emphatically that this woman had seven devils in her. Jesus cast them out, and she became His disciple. This is conclusive proof that humans can have evil spirits in them and that Christ can cast them out.

2) Luke 4:33 tells about Jesus' going to worship. In the synagogue was a demon-possessed man. This devil felt very comfortable in the church until Jesus arrived. He enjoyed the dead sermons and lifeless prayers.

56

Luke 4:33, *And in the synagogue there was a man, which had a spirit of an unclean devil, and cried out with a loud voice.*

But when our Lord walked in, the devil began to scream at Him and said in Luke 4:34, *. . .I know thee who thou art; the Holy One of God. And Jesus said, . . .Come out!* Instantly the man was delivered of the unclean spirit. Times have not changed. There are still people loitering around churches who need to be set free from the devil's power.

3) An amazing deliverance in the Bible is the healing of the demoniac of Gadara. The Bible says that this man possessed one legion of bad spirits. "Legion" is a Roman military term for a force of between two and six thousand men. The man of Gadara possessed that many evil spirits within him. Spirits do not necessarily need space as things do in the physical world. I presume a million evil spirits could be in one place because they do not need physical room. For this reason, thousands could be inside one physical being.

4) Jesus cast demons out of multitudes of people.

Matthew 8:16, *When the even was come, they brought unto him many that were possessed with devils: and he cast out the spirits with his word, and healed all that were sick.*

Luke 4:41, *And devils also came out of many, crying out, and saying, Thou art Christ the Son of God. And he rebuking them suffered them not to speak: for they knew that he was Christ.*

2. THE GIVEN POWER

Perhaps someone will say, "But that was Jesus, and He hasn't lived on this earth for two thousand years." Permit me to direct your attention to Luke 9:1, *Then he called his twelve disciples together, and gave them power and authority over all devils. . .*

This means there was no devil who could stand against these selected disciples of the Lord Jesus Christ who were to go in His name to set humanity free.

The seventy were given power.

Luke 10:1-17, *After these things the Lord appointed other seventy also, and sent them two and two before his face into every city and place, whither he himself would come.*
v. 2, *Therefore said he unto them, The harvest truly is great, but the labourers are few: pray ye therefore the Lord of the harvest, that he would send forth labourers into his harvest.*
v. 3, *Go your ways: behold, I send you forth as lambs among wolves.*
v. 4, *Carry neither purse, nor scrip, nor shoes: and salute no man by the way.*
v. 5, *And into whatsoever house ye enter, first say, Peace be to this house.*

v. 6, *And if the son of peace be there, your peace shall rest upon it: if not, it shall turn to you again.*

v. 7, *And in the same house remain, eating and drinking such things as they give: for the labourer is worthy of his hire. Go not from house to house.*

v. 8, *And into whatsoever city ye enter, and they receive you, eat such things as are set before you:*

v. 9, *And heal the sick that are therein, and say unto them, The kingdom of God is come nigh unto you.*

v. 10, *But into whatsoever city ye enter, and they receive you not, go your ways out into the streets of the same, and say,*

v. 11, *Even the very dust of your city, which cleaveth on us, we do wipe off against you: notwithstanding be ye sure of this, that the kingdom of God is come nigh unto you.*

v. 12, *But I say unto you, that it shall be more tolerable in that day for Sodom, than for that city.*

v. 13, *Woe unto thee, Chorazin! woe unto thee, Bethsaida! for if the mighty works had been done in Tyre and Sidon, which have been done in you, they had a great while ago repented, sitting in sackcloth and ashes.*

v. 14, *But it shall be more tolerable for Tyre and Sidon at the judgment, than for you.*

v. 15, *And thou, Capernaum, which art exalted to heaven, shalt be thrust down to hell.*

v. 16, *He that heareth you heareth me; and he that despiseth you despiseth me; and he that despiseth me despiseth him that sent me.*

v. 17, *And the seventy returned again with joy, saying, Lord, even the devils are subject unto us through thy name.*

Again, someone will say, "But that was the disciples. That was a long time ago." May I refer you further to Mark 16:17, *And these signs shall follow them that believe; In my name shall they cast out devils; they shall speak with new tongues.*

In The Great Commission of our Lord and Savior Jesus Christ, He commanded the people who were to come after Him (anybody who believed upon Him) to take power over demon spirits and cast them out in His name. In these last days, there will be multitudes of people needing to be set free. The church must gird itself for the greatest battle in history against demon power. The battle will be greater than it ever has been in the past. Demons will try in a greater measure to take over human beings. God's children must stand up against them. We must believe for a tremendous victory.

As Christians, we need not fear any work of the devil. We have no reason for fear. The Bible says in James 4:7, *. . .resist the devil and he will flee from you. . .* It does not say that he will walk or crawl. It says he will flee. No one flees unless he is afraid. If the devil is afraid of the true child of God, why should the Christian be afraid? There is no need for both to be afraid.

One of the great truths of the Bible is that God's children have no reason to fear any aspect of demon power. We can all be set free and we can set others free by His great power (See I John 4:4).

NOTES

_____

_____

_____

_____

_____

_____

_____

_____

_____

_____

_____

_____

_____

_____

_____

_____

_____

_____

_____

_____

_____

_____

_____

_____

INDIANA CHRISTIAN UNIVERSITY

DEMONOLOGY & DELIVERANCE I

Lesson 12

DEMON SPIRITS WORKING IN THE OLD TESTAMENT

INTRODUCTION:

From the Garden of Eden the devil has fomented revolt and rebellion against God. He has caused confusion and chaos from generation to generation.

From Genesis to Malachi God warned His people to be free of demon power. He had His prophets write it down.

1.   MOSES WARNED AGAINST WITCHCRAFT

Deuteronomy 18:10-13, *There shall not be found among you any one that maketh his son or his daughter to pass through the fire, or that useth divination, or an observer of times, or an enchanter, or a witch,*
v. 11, *Or a charmer, or a consulter with familiar spirits, or a wizard, or a necromancer.*
v. 12, *For all that do these things are an abomination unto the LORD: and because of these abominations the LORD thy God doth drive them out from before thee.*
v. 13, *Thou shalt be perfect with the LORD thy God.*

2.   THE DEATH PENALTY FOR WITCHCRAFT

Leviticus 20:6, *And the soul that turneth after such as have familiar spirits, and after wizards, to go a-whoring after them, I will even set my face against that soul, and will cut him off from among his people.*

3. THE NATION OF ISRAEL FORSOOK GOD TO WORSHIP DEVILS

Deuteronomy 32:17, *They sacrificed unto devils, not to God; to gods whom they knew not, to new gods that came newly up, whom your fathers feared not.*

4. A KING LED THE PEOPLE TO DEVIL WORSHIP

2 Chronicles 11:15, *And he ordained him priests for the high places, and for the devils, and for the calves which he had made.*

5. THE DEVIL SOUGHT TO DESTROY ISRAEL

1 Chronicles 21:1, *And Satan stood up against Israel, and provoked David to number Israel.*

6. THE DEVIL ASSAILED A GOOD MAN

Job 1:6-12, *Now there was a day when the sons of God came to present themselves before the LORD, and Satan came also among them.* (Revelation 12:10).
v. 7, *And the LORD said unto Satan, Whence comest thou? Then Satan answered the LORD, and said, From going to and fro in the earth, and from walking up and down in it.*
v. 8, *And the LORD said unto Satan, Hast thou considered my servant Job, that there is none like him in the earth, a perfect and an upright man, one that feareth God, and escheweth evil?*
v. 9, *Then Satan answered the LORD, and said, Doth Job fear God for nought?*
v. 10, *Hast not thou made an hedge about him, and about his house, and about all that he hath on every side? thou hast blessed the work of his hands, and his substance is increased in the land.*
v. 11, *But put forth thine hand now, and touch all that he hath, and he will curse thee to thy face.*
v. 12, *And the LORD said unto Satan, Behold, all that he hath is in thy power; only upon himself put not forth thine hand. So Satan went forth from the presence of the LORD.*

7. SATAN ACCUSED JOB AND ATTACKED HIM

Job 2:1-7, *Again there was a day when the sons of God came to present themselves before the LORD, and Satan came also among them to present himself before the LORD.*
v. 2, *And the LORD said to Satan, From whence comest thou? And Satan answered the LORD, and said, From going to and fro in the earth, and from walking up and down in it.*

v. 3, *And the LORD said to Satan, Hast thou considered my servant Job, that there is none like him in the earth, a perfect and an upright man, one that feareth God, and escheweth evil? and still he holdeth fast his integrity, although you movedst me against him, to destroy him without cause.*

v. 4, *And Satan answered the LORD, and said, Skin for skin, yea, all that a man hath will he give for his life.*

v. 5, *But put forth thine hand now, and touch his bone and his flesh, and he will curse thee to thy face.*

v. 6, *And the LORD said to Satan, Behold, he is in thine hand; but save his life.*

v. 7, *So went Satan forth from the presence of the LORD, and smote Job with sore boils from the sole of his foot unto his crown.*

8. THE DEVIL WITHSTOOD THE HIGH PRIEST

Zechariah 3:1, *And he showed me Joshua the high priest standing before the angel of the LORD, and Satan standing at his right hand to resist him.*

9. GOD WARNED HIS PEOPLE

Isaiah 8:19-22, *And when they shall say unto you, Seek unto them that have familiar spirits, and unto wizards that peep, and that mutter: should not a people seek unto their God? for the living to the dead?*

v. 20, *To the law and to the testimony: if they speak not according to this word, it is because there is no light in them.*

v. 21, *And they shall pass through it, hardly bestead and hungry: and it shall come to pass, that when they shall be hungry, they shall fret themselves, and curse their king and their God, and look upward.*

v. 22, *And they shall look unto the earth; and behold trouble and darkness, dimness of anguish; and they shall be driven to darkness.*

10. A NATION LEARNED THE HARD WAY

Leviticus 17:7, *And they shall no more offer their sacrifices unto devils, after whom they have gone a-whoring. This shall be a statute for ever unto them throughout their generations.*

11. THE DEVIL'S STRATEGY

I Kings 22:20-24, *And the LORD said, Who shall persuade Ahab, that he may go up and fall at Ramoth-gilead? And one said on this manner, and another said on that manner.*

v. 21, *And there came forth a spirit, and stood before the LORD, and said, I will persuade him.*

v. 22, *And the LORD said unto him, Wherewith? And he said, I will go forth, and I will be a lying spirit in the mouth of all his prophets. And he said, Thou shalt persuade him, and prevail also: go forth, and do so.*

v. 23, *Now therefore, behold, the LORD hath put a lying spirit in the mouth of all these thy prophets, and the LORD hath spoken evil concerning thee.*

v. 24, *But Zedekiah the son of Chenaanah went near, and smote Micaiah on the cheek, and said, Which way went the spirit of the LORD from me to speak unto thee?*

DEMONOLOGY & DELIVERANCE I

Lesson 13

CHRIST AND DEMONS

INTRODUCTION:

Christ in His life and ministry constantly dealt with the devil and demons.

1. INDIRECT WARFARE

    A.   It began in infancy when Herod killed all the children of Bethlehem two years old and under. He was seeking to kill the Christ Child.

        Matthew 2:16, *Then Herod, when he saw that he was mocked of the wise men, was exceeding wroth, and sent forth, and slew all the children that were in Bethlehem, and in all the coasts thereof, from two years old and under, according to the time which he had diligently inquired of the wise men.*

    B.   The people of Nazareth tried to throw Him off a precipice. He had spoken gracious words to them (Luke 4:14-21), but then they voiced the excuse of unbelief, "Is not this Joseph's son?" (Luke 4:22). They were not prepared to yield to His claim that the prophetic Isaiah scripture was being fulfilled in their midst. His words angered them. The devil seized it as an opportunity to try and get rid of Jesus.

        Luke 4:28-30, *And all they in the synagogue, when they heard these things, were filled with wrath,*
        v. 29, *And rose up, and thrust him out of the city, and led him unto the brow of the hill whereon their city was built, that they might cast him down headlong.*
        v. 30, *But he passing through the midst of them went his way.*

C.   While He slept, the devil sought to drown Him in a storm.

Mark 4:37-41, *And there arose a great storm of wind, and the waves beat into the ship, so that it was now full.*
v. 38, *And he was in the hinder part of the ship, alseep on a pillow: and they awake him, and say unto him, Master, carest thou not that we perish?*
v. 39, *And he arose, and rebuked the wind, and said unto the sea, Peace, be still. And the wind ceased, and there was a great calm.*
v. 40, *And he said unto them, Why are ye so fearful? how is it that ye have no faith?*
v. 41, *And they feared exceedingly, and said one to another, What manner of man is this, that even the wind and the sea obey him?*

D.   The demoniac of Gadara confronted Jesus as soon as He got out of the boat.

Mark 5:2-9, *And when he was come out of the ship, immediately there met him out of the tombs a man with an unclean spirit,*
v. 3, *Who had his dwelling among the tombs; and no man could bind him, no, not with chains.*
v. 4, *Because that he had been often bound with fetters and chains, and the chains had been plucked asunder by him, and the fetters broken in pieces: neither could any man tame him.*
v. 5, *And always, night and day, he was in the mountains, and in the tombs, crying, and cutting himself with stones.*
v. 6, *But when he saw Jesus afar off, he ran and worshipped him,*
v. 7, *And cried with a loud voice, and said, What have I to do with thee, Jesus, thou Son of the most high God? I adjure thee by God, that thou torment me not.*
v. 8, *For he said unto him, Come out of the man, thou unclean spirit.*
v. 9, *And he asked him, What is thy name? And he answered, saying, My name is Legion: for we are many.*

E.   The hatred and death plot of the Pharisees proved that the devil wanted Jesus dead.

Matthew 26:3-4, *Then assembled together the chief priests, and the scribes, and the elders of the people, unto the palace of the high priest, who was called Caiaphas.*
v. 4, *And consulted that they might take Jesus by subtlety, and kill him.*

2.   DIRECT CONFRONTATIONS

Christ was attacked by the devil three times in direct confrontation.

A. The first attack was in the area of self-preservation.

Matthew 4:3, *And when the tempter came to him, he said, If thou be the Son of God, command that these stones be made bread.*

B. The second attack was in the area of self-adulation.

Matthew 4:6, *And saith unto him, If thou be the Son of God, cast thyself down: for it is written, He shall give his angels charge concerning thee; and in their hands they shall bear thee up, lest at any time thou dash thy foot against a stone.*

C. The third attack was in the area of self-glorification.

Matthew 4:8-9, *Again, the devil taketh him up into an exceeding high mountain, and sheweth him all the kingdoms of the world, and the glory of them.*
v. 9, *And saith unto him, All these things will I give thee, if thou wilt fall down and worship me.*

3. CHRIST IDENTIFIED DEMON SPIRITS

A. Deaf and dumb spirits

A father brought his son who had a mute spirit to Jesus (Mark 9:17). He begged Jesus to have compassion and help them (v. 22).

Mark 9:25, *. . .Jesus . . . rebuked the foul spirit, saying unto him, Thou dumb and deaf spirit, I charge thee, come out of him, and enter no more into him.*

B. Infirmity

Luke 13:11-13, *And, behold, there was a woman which had a spirit of infirmity eighteen years, and was bowed together, and could in no wise lift up herself.*
v. 12, *And when Jesus saw her, he called her to him, and said unto her, Woman, thou art loosed from thine infirmity.*
v. 13, *And he laid his hands on her: and immediately she was made straight, and glorified God.*

4. CHRIST KNEW THE NUMBER OF DEMONS IN A PERSON

A. One

Mark 1:26, *And when the unclean spirit had torn him, and cried with a loud voice, he came out of him.*

B. Many

Mark 1:32, 34, *And at even, when the sun did set, they brought unto him all that were diseased, and them that were possessed with devils.*
v. 34, *And he healed many that were sick of divers diseases, and cast out many devils; and suffered not the devils to speak, because they knew him.*

C. Legions

Mark 5:9, *And he asked him, What is thy name? And he answered, saying, My name is Legion: for we are many.*

5. CHRIST WAS A MASTER OVER ALL DEVILS AND DEMONS

A. They feared Him and confessed His power.

Matthew 8:29, *And, behold, they cried out, saying, What have we to do with thee, Jesus, thou Son of God? art thou come hither to torment us before the time?*

B. They confessed His power to incarcerate them (Matthew 8:29).

C. They confessed His power to destroy them (Matthew 8:29).

Christ's last command, The Great Commission, gave His disciples the authority to exorcise demons.

DEMONOLOGY & DELIVERANCE I

Lesson 14

THE CHRISTIAN'S AUTHORITY OVER DEMONS

INTRODUCTION:

Adam was created with dominion. He yielded to Satan, lost his dominion, and became a fallen creature.

Genesis 1:26-27, *And God said, Let us make man in our image, after our likeness: and let them have dominion over the fish of the sea, and over the fowl of the air, and over the cattle, and over all the earth, and over every creeping thing that creepeth upon the earth.*
v. 27, *So God created man in his own image, in the image of God created he him; male and female created he them.*

READING:

Throughout the Bible we are made aware that we are to have dominion.

Psalm 8:5-8, *For thou hast made him a little lower than the angels, and hast crowned him with glory and honour.*
v. 6, *Thou madest him to have dominion over the works of thy hands; thou hast put all things under his feet:*
v. 7, *All sheep and oxen, yea, and the beasts of the field;*
v. 8, *The fowl of the air, and the fish of the sea, and whatsoever passeth through the paths of the seas.*

Hebrews 2:6-8, *But one in a certain place testified, saying, What is man, that thou art mindful of him? or the son of man, that thou visitest him?*
v. 7, *Thou madest him a little lower than the angels; thou crownedst him with glory and honour, and didst set him over the works of thy hands:*

69

v. 8, *Thou hast put all things in subjection under his feet. For in that he put all in subjection under him, he left nothing that is not put under him. But now we see not yet all things put under him.*

John 8:32-36, *And ye shall know the truth, and the truth shall make you free.*
v. 33, *They answered him, We be Abraham's seed, and were never in bondage to any man: how sayest thou, Ye shall be made free?*
v. 34, *Jesus answered them, Verily, verily, I say unto you, Whosoever committeth sin is the servant of sin.*
v. 35, *And the servant abideth not in the house for ever: but the Son abideth ever.*
v. 36, *If the Son therefore shall make you free, ye shall be free indeed.*

1. THE CHURCH UNDER DIVINE COMMAND

    A. Mark 16:15-17, *And he said unto them, Go ye into all the world, and preach the gospel to every creature.*
        v. 16, *He that believeth and is baptized shall be saved; but he that believeth not shall be damned.*
        v. 17, *And these signs shall follow them that believe; In my name shall they cast out devils; they shall speak with new tongues.*

    B. As you have received the gift, so give. Every generation is under the divine command.

        1 Peter 4:10, *As every man hath received the gift, even so minister the same one to another, as good stewards of the manifold grace of God.*

2. CHRISTIAN AUTHORITY CHALLENGED BY THE DEVIL

    A. 1 Timothy 4:1, *Now the Spirit speaketh expressly, that in the latter times some shall depart from the faith, giving heed to seducing spirits, and doctrines of devils.*

    B. Heresies are false doctrines from the devil.

    C. Fear is a spirit. It is not based on truth; therefore, it is a seducing spirit.

    D. These are the latter times and many have departed from their original faith in God.

3. CHRISTIAN AUTHORITY TO RESIST

    A. Resist by faith

        I Peter 5:8-9, *Be sober, be vigilant; because your adversary the devil, as a roaring lion, walketh about, seeking whom he may devour:*

v. 9, *Whom resist stedfast in the faith, knowing that the same afflictions are accomplished in your brethren that are in the world.*

B.   Resist by the Spirit

James 4:7, *Submit yourselves therefore to God. Resist the devil, and he will flee from you.*

4.   CHRISTIAN EXORCISM IN JESUS' NAME

Dominion implies action. Dominion over Satan is every Christian's right by the blood of Jesus. We are to be radiant and forceful through Christ. God has invested dominion in His written word. We are to use it even as Jesus did. When Jesus answered Satan He said, "It is written. . . It is written. . ." In this way He defeated the devil. There is dominion power in the Word.

Hebrews 4:12, *For the word of God is quick, and powerful, and sharper than any two-edged sword, piercing even to the dividing asunder of soul and spirit, and of the joints and marrow, and is a discerner of the thoughts and intents of the heart.*

5.   SINNERS CANNOT CAST OUT DEVILS

A.   Acts 19:11-19, *And God wrought special miracles by the hands of Paul:*
v. 12, *So that from his body were brought unto the sick handkerchiefs or aprons, and the diseases departed from them, and the evil spirits went out of them.*
v. 13, *Then certain of the vagabond Jews, exorcists, took upon them to call over them which had evil spirits the name of the Lord Jesus, saying, We adjure you by Jesus whom Paul preacheth.*
v. 14, *And there were seven sons of one Sceva, a Jew, and chief of the priests, which did so.*
v. 15, *And the evil spirit answered and said, Jesus I know, and Paul I know; but who are ye?*
v. 16, *And the man in whom the evil spirit was leaped on them, and overcame them, and prevailed against them, so that they fled out of that house naked and wounded.*
v. 17, *And this was known to all the Jews and Greeks also dwelling at Ephesus; and fear fell on them all, and the name of the Lord Jesus was magnified.*
v. 18, *And many that believed came, and confessed, and shewed their deeds.*
v. 19, *Many of them also which used curious arts brought their books together, and burned them before all men: and they counted the price of them, and found it fifty thousand pieces of silver.*

B.   If sinners could exorcise evil spirits it would be a house divided against itself.

   Matthew 12:26-27, *And if Satan cast out Satan, he is divided against himself;
   how shall then his kingdom stand?*
   v. 27, *And if I by Beelzebub cast out devils, by whom do your children cast
   them out? therefore they shall be your judges.*

DEMONOLOGY & DELIVERANCE I

Lesson 15

DEMON SPIRITS CAUSE SICKNESS AND DISEASE

INTRODUCTION:

There is infallible proof that evil spirits or demons bring disease and sickness upon the human body. All medical doctors find baffling cases which cannot be explained medically.

1. BODY SORES

    A. Satan caused terrible sores to be upon Job's body. No medicine of any kind could heal him. Job had no physical disability and no organ malfunctions. It was a direct work of the devil.

        Job 2:7, *So went Satan forth from the presence of the LORD, and smote Job with sore boils from the sole of his foot unto his crown.*

    B. God became Job's physician and healer.

        Job 42:10, *And the LORD turned the captivity of Job, when he prayed for his friends: also the LORD gave Job twice as much as he had before.*

2. DEAFNESS AND DUMBNESS

    Not all deafness or dumbness can be labeled demon power, but God's Word declares there are specific cases caused by demons.

    A. Matthew 9:32-33, *As they went out, behold, they brought to him a dumb man possessed with a devil.*
        v. 33, *And when the devil was cast out, the dumb spake: and the multitudes marvelled, saying, It was never so seen in Israel.*

B.   Mark 9:25, *When Jesus saw that the people came running together, he rebuked the foul spirit, saying unto him, Thou dumb and deaf spirit, I charge thee, come out of him, and enter no more into him.*

3.   BACK BOWED FOR EIGHTEEN YEARS

Luke 13:11-16, *And, behold, there was a woman which had a spirit of infirmity eighteen years, and was bowed together, and could in no wise lift up herself.*
v. 12, *And when Jesus saw her, he called her to him, and said unto her, Woman, thou art loosed from thine infirmity.*
v. 13, *And he laid his hands on her: and immediately she was made straight, and glorified God.*
v. 14, *And the ruler of the synagogue answered with indignation, because that Jesus had healed on the sabbath day, and said unto the people, There are six days in which men ought to work: in them therefore come and be healed, and not on the sabbath day.*
v. 15, *The Lord then answered him, and said, Thou hypocrite, doth not each one of you on the sabbath loose his ox or his ass from the stall, and lead him away to watering?*
v. 16, *And ought not this woman, being a daughter of Abraham, whom Satan hath bound, lo, these eighteen years, be loosed from this bond on the sabbath day?*

4.   INSANITY, LUNACY, EPILEPSY

Matthew 17:15, *Lord, have mercy on my son: for he is lunatic, and sore vexed: for ofttimes he falleth into the fire, and oft into the water.*

5.   WILD STRENGTH -- MANIAC

Mark 5:3-4, *Who had his dwelling among the tombs; and no man could bind him, no, not with chains:*
v. 4, *Because that he had been often bound with fetters and chains, and the chains had been plucked asunder by him, and the fetters broken in pieces: neither could any man tame him.*

6.   BLINDNESS

Matthew 12:22, *Then was brought unto him one possessed with a devil, blind, and dumb: and he healed him, insomuch that the blind and dumb both spake and saw.*

7.   GRIEVOUS VEXATION

Matthew 15:22, *And, behold, a woman of Canaan came out of the same coasts, and cried unto him, saying, Have mercy on me, O Lord, thou son of David; my daughter is grievously vexed with a devil.*

8. UNCLEANNESS

Luke 4:36, *And they were all amazed, and spake among themselves, saying, What a word is this! for with authority and power he commandeth the unclean spirits, and they come out.*

9. CONVULSIONS

Mark 9:20, *Then they brought him to Him. And when he saw Him, immediately the spirit convulsed him, and he fell on the ground and wallowed, foaming at the mouth* (NKJV).

10. LUST AND A LYING SPIRIT

John 8:44, *Ye are of your father the devil, and the lusts of your father ye will do. He was a murderer from the beginning, and abode not in the truth, because there is no truth in him. When he speaketh a lie, he speaketh of his own: for he is a liar, and the father of it.*

11. GENERAL SICKNESS

Matthew 4:23-24, *And He went about all Galilee, teaching in their synagogues and preaching the good news Gospel of the kingdom and healing every disease and every weakness and infirmity among the people.*
v. 24, *So the report of Him spread throughout all Syria, and they brought Him all that were sick, those afflicted with various diseases and torments, those under the power of demons, and epileptics, and paralyzed people; and He healed them* (AMP).

12. BONDAGE

Romans 8:15, *For ye have not received the spirit of bondage again to fear; but ye have received the Spirit of adoption, whereby we cry, Abba, Father.*

13. OPPRESSION

Acts 10:38, *. . . God anointed Jesus of Nazareth with the Holy Ghost and with power: who went about doing good, and healing all that were oppressed of the devil; for God was with him.*

CONCLUSION:

John, Jesus' beloved friend and disciple, clearly defined for us what Satan and his hosts are doing. In so doing, John portrayed Jesus in the shepherd function and the devil as a thief. It is an easily understood parable.

Demon Spirits Cause Sickness and Disease
Lesson 15

John 10:10, *The thief cometh not, but for to steal, and to kill, and to destroy: I am come that they might have life, and that they might have it more abundantly.*

The devil steals health and sanity.

The devil kills by cancer and other devouring diseases.

The devil destroys spirit, soul, and body of any human who yields to his deceptions.

done yields

① STANd oN The word.

② done move

INDIANA CHRISTIAN UNIVERSITY

DEMONOLOGY & DELIVERANCE I

Lesson 16

DESTROYING THE EMBLEMS OF DEMON POWER

INTRODUCTION:

God warns His people against all supernaturalism that is not of Him. There are two areas of supernaturalism. One is demon power and the other is God's power. Anything related to demon power should have no relationship to Christians.

The Apostle Paul says that the idols and the sacrifices to idols are nothing. Behind each idol is a demon craving to be worshiped. The idol is a symbol; behind that symbol is the devil's power.

I Corinthians 10:19-20, *What say I then? that the idol is any thing, or that which is offered in sacrifice to idols is any thing?*
v. 20, *But I say, that the things which the Gentiles sacrifice, they sacrifice to devils, and not to God: and I would not that ye should have fellowship with devils.*

1.   DIVINE SYMBOLS

God has symbols of His power. In the Old Testament, there was the Ark of God. The Ark was a symbol of God's presence and power. The Ark of God was placed in the Holy of Holies. Above the Ark was the Shekinah. It was a light unlike any human light. There were no candles nor artificial light of any nature in the Holy of Holies. When the light was gone, God was gone.

Exodus 25:21-22, *And thou shalt put the mercy seat above upon the ark; and in the ark thou shalt put the testimony that I shall give thee.*
v. 22, *And there I will meet with thee, and I will continue with thee from above the mercy seat, from between the two cherubims which are upon the ark of the testimony, of all things which I will give thee in commandment unto the children of Israel.*

2. THE HEATHEN DID NOT UNDERSTAND GOD'S POWER

When the Philistines captured the Ark of God, seeing that it was a religious relic, they placed it in their temple. The next morning, their own god, Dagon, was down on his face, broken to pieces, and destroyed. The presence of God in the symbolic Ark destroyed Dagon.

1 Samuel 5:4, *And when they arose early on the morrow morning, behold, Dagon was fallen upon his face to the ground before the ark of the LORD; and the head of Dagon and both the palms of his hands were cut off upon the threshold; only the stump of Dagon was left to him.*

3. SYMBOLS OF SATANISM

The devil has symbols of his power. Christians should never have symbols of the devil's power in their possession. These symbols of the devil's power may have strength that you don't know about.

The heathen use all kinds of symbols to worship. The witch doctors of the world make dolls, usually very ugly dolls. Then by sticking pins through these dolls, they can cause injury to their enemies at a distance. The dolls become symbols of their evil practice.

All voodoo religions have artifacts. They have numerous good luck charms. They have all kinds of symbols which refer to the power of the devil.

4. COBRA IN THE CLASSROOM

A Bible school teacher in England told me that after breakfast each morning he had a class in a certain room. Each morning the students would get drowsy and go to sleep. It was abnormal. He thought maybe they were getting too much breakfast but nobody gets too much breakfast at Bible school! He began looking around the classroom and discovered a bronze serpent from India on a window ledge. It was a coiled cobra which is worshiped as a god in India. He saw this bronze cobra and said, "Well, I'll just move that thing out to the yard." He told no one about moving the idol. The next morning, not one single student became drowsy.

5. HOLE IN THE IDOL

When in China a number of years ago, I was in a large Buddhist temple. The priest showed me their gods. They had many idols. Some were frightening, others had eight or ten arms sticking out of them.

Pointing to an idol about 16 or 18 feet high I said to the priest, "How can that idol help you?"

He was very polite as he smiled and said, "You don't understand, being a foreigner.

That idol does not have power. We all know that. The spirit of that idol is elsewhere right now, but if I were to bring incense and food and place it before that idol and start praying, something would start happening."

He took me around to the back of this huge idol and pointed to a hole. "That is where the spirit goes in and out," he said. "It wants worship, and so if I come and kneel here and offer an offering and burn incense or candles, immediately the spirit comes and communicates with me."

The devil wants to be worshiped and he will get into any kind of idol if a human will worship him.

The idol was a symbol for the demon spirit. The grotesque face of that idol was something the artist conceived under the power of the devil. A Christian should have no such idols in his home.

6.   THE EVIL TREE OF LUZON

In the headhunter country of Luzon we helped to build a tribal church. While preaching there they showed me a special tree where the spirits lived. That tree was a symbol of demon power; it was greasy looking and did not have a leaf on it. I suppose that was because the worshipers had wiped their hands on it so often. In looking at the tree, there was something very strange. . .it looked evil. Even though the boughs were gnarled and crooked, it looked like a possessed tree.

The tribe said that their spirit gods lived in the tree. They came and offered their offerings and burned incense at the foot of the tree. The tree became a symbol of the devil's power.

7.   THE STRANGE CROSS

When I prayed for a possessed girl in the Philippines, Clarita Villanueva, she wore a strange metal cross around her neck. This cross was a symbol of the devil's power.

Clarita sometimes acted like an animal. She would crawl up under the desk of the Chief of Police. Once he kicked her and said, "Come out from under there!" She complained, "I've lost my cross." He said that he didn't know anything about her cross. To prove it he took both his front pockets and turned them wrong side out and shook them. Then he put his pockets back in and Clarita said, "Look again." The policeman plunged his hand into his pocket and found that her metal cross was in his pocket! It frightened him. Four days, later he died.

8.   THE SATAN SWORD

When I preached in Indonesia, I stayed in the home of a lay witch doctor; he was possessed of seven devils. While he was at work one day, his wife showed me how he communicated with his spirits. These spirits hated his wife because she was

Christian. She even had to sleep in another room for when she tried to sleep with her husband, these spirits threw her onto the floor. She had black and blue marks on her body as a result. Now you may not understand things like that, but a lot of people in America are beginning to understand things that they never understood before about the devil's power.

9. CRYSTAL BALL AND CARDS

You have read of Jeanne Dixon in Washington, D.C. She prognosticates the future for politicians and others.

In order to predict the future or anything about someone, Mrs. Dixon uses a crystal ball. She also uses a deck of cards for fortune telling. That crystal ball and deck of cards is a symbol of the devil's power.

Do you have a ouija board at your house? If you do, take it out and burn it in Jesus' name, because it is a symbol of the devil's power.

It may be that you have some professional playing cards. Almost every witch doctor and fortuneteller in the whole world uses them. They help them in their business. If that is true, you have no business with cards in your house!

It might be that you have a crystal ball at your house. It may be a toy or a plaything; it has no business in your house. You ought to destroy it.

10. HEATHEN CURIOS

On your "whatnot" shelf you might have little idols purchased in department stores in this country today. You can buy almost any heathen idol in the department stores in America.

You might have brought some of these curios from foreign lands and have them placed around your house. I know in many homes where I have gone I have seen these idols of Buddha and Confucius. I don't believe that they should be there. They may not have hurt you yet, but I believe that we should clean them out in Jesus' name.

11. GOD'S PEOPLE MUST BE CAREFUL

In the Old Testament God's people were very careful about pictures lest they be worshiped. It is very interesting that Orthodox Jews will not have their picture taken. When you go to Jerusalem, the Orthodox Jews wearing beards do not want to be photographed.

The Amish people do not want their picture taken and do not have pictures in their houses. This is because of the Second Commandment.

12. THE ANSWER

You say, "Brother Sumrall, what can we do about this?" Acts 19:19 says, *Many of them also which used curious arts brought their books together, and burned them before all men: and they counted the price of them, and found it fifty thousand pieces of silver.*

This was a fortune. At that time, thirty pieces was the price of a slave. This means that with fifty thousand pieces of silver, they could have bought one thousand, six hundred sixty-six and two-thirds slaves. There was possibly no man in the empire that wealthy.

They brought all this wealth into the streets and burned it. They took it out publicly and burned it and destroyed it so that nothing of the devil's power might remain.

The answer for us is to be certain that nothing we possess comes between us and God. Satan would like nothing better than for God's people to become so enamored with things that they forget God.

13. AMERICAN MAGIC

In America people put good luck charms in their automobiles. They hang them around their rearview mirror in order to have good luck. Many of them are symbols of demon power and should not be used. Christ said in John 4:24 that we are to worship God in Spirit and in truth. Some people have writings on pieces of paper they keep in their pockets in order to have good luck. Luck has to do with the devil. There is no good luck with God. The things that come to us from God come by God's loving care.

Anything of a superstitious nature in one's life must be cast out. Anyone who is going to fortunetellers of any kind is opening his life to demon possession.

I urge you not to read horoscopes. They are lies of the devil.

Believers must place their lives in the hand of God to guide them everyday. They don't need to know what is going to happen tomorrow. If they did, they wouldn't have to walk by faith. Christians don't need to be curiously looking into the future. The Word of God tells them all they need to know. If one believes in the Gospel, he is saved; if one doesn't, he is damned.

Mark 16:16, *He that believeth and is baptized shall be saved; but he that believeth not shall be damned.* When one dies, he will go to heaven, or he will go to hell.

We must make a crusade for clean hands, clean hearts, and clean homes. We must clear all symbols of the devil's power out of our homes. We must dig out the very roots of superstition and all that has to do with the devil's power. As we do, we will meet God in cleanliness of heart.

Two thousand years ago the Christians were very careful to clean out every symbol of the devil's power around them. You and I must do the same.

In Latin America, when they become evangelical Christians they clean out their houses. They take the images and break them to pieces. When you walk into their home, you find it cleansed of everything that had any relationship to the devil's power.

If you do have anything that needs to be cleaned out of your house, do it now! Our homes are cleansed by the blood of Jesus Christ!

DEMONOLOGY & DELIVERANCE I

Lesson 17

CAN A CHRISTIAN BE POSSESSED WITH A DEVIL? PART I

INTRODUCTION:

This is possibly the question most often asked in my seminars overseas and in the cities of America. To me it is like asking if a patriotic American soldier can become an atheistic Russian soldier. It is remarkable that this question should be a problem to Christians. Yet I have been asked by literally hundreds of people in a hundred countries and cities around the world if a Christian can be possessed with a demon spirit.

Ephesians 6:12, *For we wrestle not against flesh and blood, but against principalities, against powers, against the rulers of the darkness of this world, against spiritual wickedness in high places* (KJV).

Ours is not a conflict with mere flesh and blood; but with the depotisms; the empires, the forces that control and govern this dark world: the spiritual hosts of evil arrayed against us in heavenly warfare (Weymouth).

The adversaries with whom we wrestle are not flesh and blood, but they are the principalities, the powers, and the sovereigns of this present darkness, the spirits of evil in the heavens (Conybeare).

We have to struggle, not with blood and flesh, but with the angelic rulers, the angelic authorities, the potentates of the dark present, the spirit-forces of evil in the heavenly sphere; so take God's armour; praying. . .with all manner of prayer (Moffatt).

1. DEFINITIONS

There is a very real battle of definitions going on in the religious world. It centers around who can and who cannot be possessed of a demon. It does not matter to which church a person goes or is a member of if he or she needs deliverance from a tormenting spirit of fear or oppression of the devil. That person should be set free by a prayer of deliverance and not begin a dialogue on who can or who cannot be possessed.

2. FIRST THE POSITIVE SIDE: THE TWELVE DISCIPLES

A. I feel that the correct way to answer this question is to first state the Christian's position in Christ. When Christ sent His twelve apostles out, He gave them power and authority over devils.

Matthew 10:1, *And when he had called unto him his twelve disciples, he gave them power against unclean spirits, to cast them out, and to heal all manner of sickness and all manner of disease.*

B. Jesus did not warn the apostles to protect themselves against demon power. Above all, He did not warn them that they may become possessed or injured while rebuking demons. Jesus gave them divine authority over all demonic forces. The Bible nowhere teaches disciples to fear the devil or of a danger of personal demon possession.

3. THEN THE SEVENTY DISCIPLES CAST OUT DEVILS

When the Lord sent out His seventy disciples, He gave them explicit power not only to heal the sick, but to cast out devils.

Luke 10:17-19, *And the seventy returned again with joy, saying, Lord, even the devils are subject unto us through thy name.*
v. 18, *And he said unto them. . .*
v. 19, *Behold, I give unto you power to tread on serpents and scorpions, and over all the power of the enemy: and nothing shall by any means hurt you.*

Christ did not warn the seventy in any way to protect themselves against demon power or to be careful in the way they handled evil spirits. Jesus did not warn them of any personal danger but commanded them to cast out devils without fear, and said, *". . .nothing shall by any means hurt you."*

4. THE GREAT COMMISSION TO ALL BELIEVERS

Mark 16:17, *And these signs shall follow them that believe; In my name shall they cast out devils; they shall speak with new tongues.*

In His final commission before Christ returned to the right hand of the Father in heaven, His last instructions were to deliver people who are possessed of devils. He did not imply that these devils would hurt believers or that they would even stand up against them. He told His disciples to cast them out! The Word of God is either true or not true. If we as Christians have authority to cast out the devil, we must obey. The words "cast out" are offensive action. This means to take the initiative and be the aggressor.

NOTES

STUDY GUIDE

INDIANA CHRISTIAN UNIVERSITY

DEMONOLOGY & DELIVERANCE I

Lesson 18

CAN A CHRISTIAN BE POSSESSED WITH A DEVIL? PART II

1. THE DIVIDED KINGDOM

     A.   When Jesus was accused of using demon power to cast out devils, He said that a kingdom divided against itself could not stand.

          Matthew 12:25, *And Jesus knew their thoughts, and said unto them, Every kingdom divided against itself is brought to desolation; and every city or house divided against itself shall not stand:*

     B.   One cannot be an effective part of two opposite kingdoms. Jesus said that a man cannot serve two masters.

          Matthew 6:24, *No man can serve two masters: for either he will hate the one, and love the other; or else he will hold to the one, and despise the other. Ye cannot serve God and mammon.*

     C.   The Apostle James asked if sweet and bitter waters could come from the same fountain.

          James 3:11, *Doth a fountain send forth at the same place sweet water and bitter?*

2. THE POSITIVE ACTION

     James 4:7, *Submit yourselves therefore unto God. Resist the devil, and he will flee from you.*

There are two aspects of this verse.

A.   First is submitting ourselves to God which means that we refuse to submit to the devil's presence or his deceiving ways.

B.   Second is resist the devil. Resistance is a military action. To resist shows strength. God declares that upon this action, the devil will flee from you. To flee is not just to crawl, walk, or even run. A fleeing person runs in terror.

C.   When the devil understands that a Christian has a strong position in God and that he is actively resisting him, the Bible declares that the devil will flee. I have always found the Bible to be true.

D.   If a Christian actively, persistently, dogmatically, and spiritually resists the devil, then the Bible says that he will flee.

E.   If the devil will run from us in terror, why should Christians be afraid of him? How can he hurt them?

3. THE BATTLE ACTION: PROTECTION FOR BELIEVERS

Ephesians 6:10-12, *Finally, my brethren, be strong in the Lord, and in the power of his might.*
v. 11, *Put on the whole armour of God, that ye may be able to stand against the wiles of the devil.*
v. 12, *For we wrestle not against flesh and blood, but against principalities, against powers, against the rulers of the darkness of this world, against spiritual wickedness in high places.*

The believer's enemies are the demonic hosts of Satan, assembled for mortal combat. Verses 13 through 18 describe the Christian's armor for this warfare with Satan and his hosts.

Ephesians 6:13-18, *Wherefore take unto you the whole armour of God, that ye may be able to withstand in the evil day, and having done all, to stand.*
v. 14, *Stand therefore, having your loins girt about with truth, and having on the breastplate of righteousness;*
v. 15, *And your feet shod with the preparation of the gospel of peace;*
v. 16, *Above all, taking the shield of faith, wherewith ye shall be able to quench all the fiery darts of the wicked.*
v. 17, *And take the helmet of salvation, and the sword of the Spirit, which is the word of God:*
v. 18, *Praying always with all prayer and supplication in the Spirit, and watching thereunto with all perseverance and supplication in the Spirit, and watching thereunto with all perseverance and supplication for all saints.*

4. THE DEAF AND DUMB

This is the positive side of Christian security and power. The Lord Jesus said that he cast out a deaf spirit and He called it a spirit of deafness. He also cast out dumbness and He called it a spirit of dumbness.

Matthew 9:32-33, *As they went out, behold, they brought to him a dumb man possessed with a devil.*
v. 33, *And when the devil was cast out, the dumb spake: and the multitudes marveled, saying, It was never so seen in Israel.*

No person would, for a moment, say that all the deaf people in the world would go to hell; yet the Bible says that for some it is a spirit that has made them deaf or dumb. So, a person can be a devoted Christian and love God, yet be totally deaf. This means that forms of deafness are caused by the devil, according to the ministry of Jesus Christ.

5. HOW A CHURCH MEMBER GOT POSSESSED

How is it possible for a professing Christian to become demon possessed? A church woman suffering from the power of the devil was asked, "Evil spirit, how did you get into this woman?"

It answered back, "She came to the adult motion picture theater to see a sex movie. While she was watching, I was there and I had a right to go into her."

This opened up a tremendous avenue of thinking for me. If Jesus were on this earth, He would not frequent theaters to be contaminated with filthy, immoral, and sensual suggestions and to listen to obscenities.

When a person deliberately goes into the devil's territory, while he is there it is possible to become a victim of whatever the devil offers, even though the person claims to be a Christian.

For example, when we lived in Hong Kong we had the full protection of American might and of British strength as long as we stayed on the right side of the border. I looked across the China border many times, but I never wanted to go into Communist China. If I had crossed that border my protection rights would have ceased. The same is true of Christian living.

Cross over into the devil's territory, and you may pay a severe price.

6. HOW A PERSON YIELDS TO DEMON POWER

A. I am personally convinced that anger can be a spirit and can actually make a person insane. In Denver, Colorado, I was asked to pray for a man in a nursing home who was paralyzed. I was told that his condition was the result of a fit of rage.

89

B. While praying for a motion picture actor in Manila who had suffered two strokes, his wife said that both strokes came upon him during a violent fit of anger.

C. I am convinced that adultery is a spirit. Multitudes of people testify that the demonic urge of adultery overwhelms them. One man told me that cold perspiration dropped from his fingers and he trembled all over until he stopped resisting and submitted to the evil spirit, yet he was a prominent church worker.

D. This means that a professing church member can open the doors of his soul and spirit to lust, jealousy, or lying.

Paul said in 2 Timothy 2:24-26, *And the servant of the Lord must not strive; but be gentle unto all men, apt to teach, patient,*
v. 25, *In meekness instructing those that oppose themselves; if God peradventure will give them repentance to the acknowledging of the truth;*
v. 26, *And that they may recover themselves out of the snare of the devil, who are taken captive by him at his will.*

7. MY "OLD" ANSWER

Can a Christian become demon possessed? For many years I have said "unequivocally no," but after meeting so many people who claim to be Christians and seeing them under the power of the devil, I had to come up with some answers. People who claim to know God but live a fleshly, carnal life, open the doors of their heart, spirit, soul, and mind to the devil; he takes advantage of them and dominates them through evil desires. They find themselves in the clutches of the devil and they can only be set free by the power of God.

8. THE "WORD" ANSWER   *Key*

A. The Bible, God's Word, says in Ephesians 5:18, *Be filled with the Spirit, and in so doing you give no place to the devil.* Those who do not follow this command to be filled with the Spirit give place to the devil to enter their lives.

B. If a person who claims to be a Christian dabbles with the occult, he can become demon possessed.

isA

1 Timothy 4:1, *Now the Spirit speaketh expressly, that in the latter times some shall depart from the faith, giving heed to seducing spirits, and doctrines of devils.*

I have met many.

C. If a church member lies like Ananias and Sapphira lied in Acts 5:1-11, he gives room to Satan.

Acts 5:3, *But Peter said, Ananias, why hath Satan filled thine heart to lie to the Holy Ghost, and to keep back part of the price of the land?*

D. If a professed Christian betrays truth as Judas did, he certainly opens his being to satanic possession.

Luke 22:3, *Then entered Satan into Judas surnamed Iscariot, being of the number of the twelve.*

E. Simon, a sorcerer, was apparently among those participating in the revival in Samaria.

Acts 8:13, *Then Simon himself believed also: and when he was baptized, he continued with Philip, and wondered, beholding the miracles and signs which were done.*

He believed. He was baptized. He continued with Philip. However, in Acts 8:23, Peter said he was in the "bond of iniquity."

Acts 8:23, *For I percieve that thou art in the gall of bitterness, and in the bond of iniquity.*

Peter told Simon that his heart was not right with God (v. 21). He was told to repent and seek God's forgiveness (v. 22).

F. The man in the synagogue, a place of religion, needed deliverance.

Mark 1:23, *And there was in their synagogue a man with an unclean spirit; and he cried out.*

G. King Saul was a spiritual man. He prophesied with the prophets. The Word says that he turned his back and had a changed heart (I Samuel 10:9), but yet Saul died because of his involvement in witchcraft.

1 Samuel 28:7, *Then said Saul unto his servants, Seek me a woman that hath a familiar spirit, that I may go to her, and inquire of her. And his servants said to him, Behold, there is a woman that hath a familiar spirit at Endor.*

NOTES

INDIANA CHRISTIAN UNIVERSITY

DEMONOLOGY & DELIVERANCE I

Lesson 19

HOW I LEARNED EXORCISM OF DEVILS PART I

INTRODUCTION:

A. God solemnly warns mankind about worshipping devils:

1 Corinthians 10:20, *But I say, that the things which the Gentiles sacrifice, they sacrifice to devils, and not to God: and I would not that ye should have fellowship with devils.*

God refuses to permit His worshipers to have fellowship of any kind with the devil or with any of his angels or any of his works.

B. There is a pertinent truth in 2 Timothy 2:26, *And that they may recover themselves out of the snare of the devil, who are taken captive by him at his will.*

This possibly refers to heathen nations. It is possible to recover them from the snare of the devil through the preaching of the gospel of Jesus Christ.

As you know, a snare is a trap, a contraption you set for a rabbit or a squirrel. The animal thinks that it is finding food to eat. Going into the trap or snare, it is caught. This is the manner in which the devil deceives the whole world, the heathen, and the people in Christian lands--by a snare. He fools them into believing that they will have pleasure, but they do not get pleasure. He fools them into believing if they follow him everything will be all right, but it is not all right. The Scripture further says that he takes them captive at his own will. That statement indicates that the devil willfully and deliberately sets snares to capture human beings.

Though I was reared in an evangelical church and environment and had seen the sick prayed for many times, I cannot remember hearing a sermon on the casting out of devils. If a person became mentally uncontrollable he was sent to the insane asylum. For some strange reason we saw no relationship between divine healing and mental illness. Not having heard a sermon on deliverance of the mentally disturbed nor having received any instruction on what to do for a demon-possessed person, I was completely uninitiated.

1. GIRL IN JAVA

It was in Indonesia on the island of Java, where I was first confronted with a demon-possessed person. We had recently arrived in the country and this was the first meeting in this city. The service was in the Javanese language. Although I could understand the melody of some of the songs, I could not understand the words being sung. As the first song was being sung I noticed a girl who was about twelve years of age get off the front bench onto the floor and start writhing like a serpent. It seemed as if I was the only one concerned about it. The congregation kept singing and the song leader did not even look. Green foam began to come out of her mouth, covering her chin and up to her nose. This did not seem to bother anyone either.

I presumed that this was something that had happened previously. There were more than six hundred people in the meeting hall and no one seemed concerned about the girl on the floor who looked like a snake with green foam coming out of her mouth. She would look up at the platform, grin a silly grin, her eyes would dance like a serpent's eyes, and foam would belch out of her mouth. She would move down three or four feet, wiggle around, and move back three or four feet on the floor. This went on for some thirty minutes during the preliminaries of the meeting. It seemed as if the girl was completely ignored. However, within me something strong was building up to a bursting point. I knew that I must meet this challenge of the devil.

When I was asked to preach, my interpreter and I walked toward the pulpit, but rather than greeting the people, words burst from my mouth, loud and clear. I cried, "Get up and sit down!" My interpreter was so startled that he did not respond. The girl was illiterate and knew no English; therefore, the only one who could have understood me would have been the spirit within her. Instantly, the girl wiped her mouth with her arm, removing the green foam. She stood up and sat down on the bench like a mummy and did not move a muscle while I preached for forty-five minutes. At the end of my sermon and without premeditation, I looked at the girl and said, "Come out of her! Be free in Jesus' name!" Instantly that transfixed look left her. That rigidity left her body. She relaxed, she smiled, she looked around, and a wave of glory went over the congregation as they saw the girl become normal. Again, my interpreter, being astounded at what happened never said a word. It, therefore, was the spirit who understood what I had said.

Later I sought to evaluate this new experience. I knew that it brought deliverance to the meeting, because when the girl sat on the bench and obeyed me it brought the entire congregation to a place of readiness to listen. When I commanded her to be free, it brought a tremendous victory into the meeting and people were ready to throng to the front to receive Christ as their Savior.

I talked to Rev. Howard Carter about this, as he was not in the meeting with me, and he told me of other instances where he had seen spirits cast out of people immediately. We began to discuss this subject more between us. However, we were now in a land of deep witchcraft. In that land, curses were put upon people and black magic was prevalent in every village. Almost daily and nightly we met situations of demon power which we had not come up against in Christianized lands.

2. BLACK AND WHITE ANGELS IN JAVA

A few nights later I was walking into a meeting in another town in Java. Again, the building was crowded with people. Every place was taken and extra chairs had been put down the aisles. As I came in the front door to walk the length of the crowded church, a woman seated in one of the extra chairs in the aisle took hold of my sleeve and tugged it gently. She looked up at me and grinned saying, "Sir, you have a little black angel in you, and I have a white angel in me."

Now I could have shook her off and gone on toward the front of the platform or I could have smiled and walked away, but something within me revolted. I turned to her quickly and said, "That is a lie. I have a white spirit within me, the Spirit of Jesus Christ, and you have a devil within you, which is black and dark. I command you to come out of her!" As I said this, I laid my hands upon her and her eyes glared strangely; her face contorted and suddenly she was released. Everyone in the area felt the release of the woman as they saw her countenance change. Rather than continuing to the front of the church, I asked through my interpreter, "How long have you been bound by the devil?"

She said, "Fifteen years ago I went to the witchdoctor and the spirit has been in me ever since. I am free now."

This seemed a strange confrontation with the devil as I had never been in this church, and I was only walking in the door when met with this situation. Yet, I felt that if I ignored it I would be defeated in my preaching. I knew that this spirit would rise up against me during the sermon and that the only means of victory was to face it and win the battle. I did not have time to consider whether I was capable of doing it. I did not have time to consider whether it was the right thing to do. I did not have time to consult with anyone as to what was wrong with the woman. I did not consider her to be out of order in any way. It simply seemed that there was an inevitable battle that must be fought on that battleground, and there could be no victory for the cause of

Christ unless I was willing to do battle. Therefore, before I reached the platform, we had to fight. The wonderful thing is that it brought tremendous release to the whole meeting. When the people saw that the visitor among them was not afraid of evil, it brought a great feeling of victory to every part of the service. Many were set free from demon power.

3. NOT A HUMAN BATTLE

We ministered for three months throughout the island of Java and we had a number of encounters with the devil. The things that we learned were most interesting. The greatest thing we learned was that it was not me, personally, in the conflict. It was something within me, which was Christ. It was not the person that I met who caused the battle. It was something within him or her, the devil.

4. NO FEAR

I discovered that there was no reason for fear because I did not lose the battles. I found that though they would scream and tear themselves, they did not seek to harm or touch me, and that I was perfectly safe in exorcising demons. I found in most cases that the demons wanted to run away and not confront me.

As I sought to confirm this activity by the Word of God, the Great Commission of our Lord Jesus commanding His disciples to cast out devils became my Gibraltar.

Mark 16:15-17, *He said unto them, Go ye into all the world, and preach the gospel to every creature.*

v. 16, *He that believeth and is baptized shall be saved; but he that believeth not shall be damned.*

v. 17, *And these signs shall follow them that believe; In my name shall they cast out devils; they shall speak with new tongues.*

STUDY GUIDE

INDIANA CHRISTIAN UNIVERSITY

DEMONOLOGY & DELIVERANCE I

Lesson 20

HOW I LEARNED EXORCISM OF DEVILS PART II

1.   PROJECTED TRUTH

The Word of God specifically says in 1 Timothy 4:1, *. . .the Spirit speaketh expressly, that in the latter times some shall depart from the faith, giving heed to seducing spirits, and doctrines of devils.*

The prophecy includes a time element. It says "latter times." These words were spoken by the Holy Spirit for the church. We are living in those latter times right now. He tells us that some shall depart from the faith. Rather than becoming a backslider or wayward in their spiritual lives, they will actually give themselves over to *seducing spirits and doctrines of devils.*

Living in the last days, we are seeing these things which were prophesied actually coming to pass. Almost every day someone who is combating an evil spirit and needs help calls my office from somewhere in America. Almost every day letters come to me from those who are tormented by the devil. They need deliverance.

A.   Psychiatry cannot set them free.

B.   Philosophy cannot deliver them.

C.   Pastoral counseling cannot set them free.

But this demon-releasing power of the Holy Spirit is available to anyone who will seek it. God is no respecter of persons.

2.   THE LAST DAYS

A.   Revelation 12:12, *Therefore rejoice, ye heavens, and ye that dwell in them. Woe to the inhabiters of the earth and of the sea! for the devil is come down unto you, having great wrath, because he knoweth that he hath but a short time.*

This scripture reveals that there will be greater demon power on the earth in the ultimate days of this dispensation.

B.   There are three unclean spirits which possess the dragon, the beast and the false prophet, the trinity of hell, and God says that they are spirits of devils working miracles and will go forth to deceive the whole world. They will ultimately gather the world to Armageddon.

Revelation 16:13-16, *And I saw three unclean spirits like frogs come out of the mouth of the dragon, and out of the mouth of the beast, and out of the mouth of the false prophet.*
v. 14, *For they are the spirits of devils, working miracles, which go forth unto the kings of the earth and of the whole world, to gather them to the battle of that great day of God Almighty.*
v. 15, *Behold, I come as a thief. Blessed is he that watcheth, and keepeth his garments, lest he walk naked, and they see his shame.*
v. 16, *And he gathered them together into a place called in the Hebrew tongue Armageddon.*

C.   We read that swarms of evil creatures will come up out of the bottomless pit to torment mankind.

Revelation 9:1-11, *And the fifth angel sounded, and I saw a star fall from heaven unto the earth: and to him was given the key of the bottomless pit.*
v. 2, *And he opened the bottomless pit; and there arose a smoke out of the pit, as the smoke of a great furnace; and the sun and the air were darkened by reason of the smoke of the pit.*
v. 3, *And there came out of the smoke locusts upon the earth: and unto them was given power, as the scorpions of the earth have power.*
v. 4, *And it was commanded them that they should not hurt the grass of the earth, neither any green thing, neither any tree; but only those men which have not the seal of God in their foreheads.*
v. 5, *And to them it was given that they should not kill them, but that they should be tormented five months: and their torment was as the torment of a scorpion, when he striketh a man.*
v. 6, *And in those days shall men seek death, and shall not find it; and shall desire to die, and death shall flee from them.*

v. 7, *And the shapes of the locusts were like unto horses prepared unto battle; and on their heads were as it were crowns like gold, and their faces were as the faces of men.*
v. 8, *And they had hair as the hair of women, and their teeth were as the teeth of lions.*
v. 9, *And they had breastplates, as it were breastplates of iron; and the sound of their wings was as the sound of chariots of many horses running to battle.*
v. 10, *And they had tails like unto scorpions, and there were stings in their tails; and their power was to hurt men five months.*
v. 11, *And they had a king over them, which is the angel of the bottomless pit, whose name in the Hebrew tongue is Abaddon, but in the Greek tongue hath his name Apollyon.*

It seems to me that the greatest need in the spiritual world is for men and women to understand how to control and cast out devils.

The church has tried to taboo the ministry of exorcising spirits. Ministers have tried to turn their backs on the situation and have mentally sick people committed to insane asylums in order to forget them. Yet there is an ever growing need for the ministry of setting people free in the spirit.

The Lord has spoken to me and indicated that in the future those that lead His army must not simply be those who pray for the sick, but those that can reach into the spirit of man and set him free from evil, breaking the powers of Satan in his spirit and mind.

In the world of tomorrow there will be millions needing to be set free. God is looking for men and women with courage and compassion to set humanity free. The Great Commission must come into dynamic force. We must obey the words of Christ and set men free. The Lord Jesus said, *They that have faith shall cast out devils. . .* We must do this without fear, without compromise, and without doubt. We must do this with the same great love that Jesus had in His compassion toward those whose lives had been threatened by the devil.

3.   THE BARKING SPIRIT

From my experiences in the Orient, I discovered that when I faced a deep problem and the kingdom of God was challenged, God came through and performed mighty miracles to set people free from Satan's power.

Arriving in Europe from the Orient, I was speaking at a meeting in Poland. I had never been there before and did not speak the Polish language. On the front row of the packed auditorium, sat a woman who would periodically say "Hallelujah" in a shrill, eerie voice. It cut my spirit when she would say this. I noticed that the local people did not seem to mind. Throughout the song service and prayer service the woman constantly interrupted everybody. I knew that I would not get through to those people unless she was stopped. Though she seemed to be religious, it was hindering the meeting. When I stood up to speak, rather than greeting the people, I looked down at her and said, "Would you please shut up!" My interpreter was so taken back that I had not greeted the people but had spoken to this woman, that he did not say anything. That woman, who could not understand English, began to bark like a dog. The people were amazed because they had not realized that this was an evil thing in her. In a few moments I looked down at her again and said, "Now, I command you to come out of her!" Without my getting close to the woman, she was set free by God's power. The meeting was blessed.

This is the manner in which I came to understand the exorcism of evil.

4.   THE DUMB SPIRIT

Upon my arrival in America, without seeking further experience, I immediately found people who needed to be delivered. One of my first meetings was in the St. Louis area. A pastor asked me if I would visit one of his parishioners who had not spoken in over three months. The young man came home late one night and was unable to explain why he could not speak. He refused a pencil to write about his condition. I went with the pastor to the home. Upon arrival I found this young man, who appeared to be about twenty and looked well and healthy. As we walked in the door his mother was saying, "Speak to me, son! Speak to me, son! Oh, please speak to me, son!" He simply glared at her. Then the mother explained his condition to me. "Our son has not spoken in over three months and we don't know why. He eats well, he sleeps well, but he won't speak."

The young man looked at me with the craziest grin you could ever imagine and I realized immediately this was a spirit that had attached itself to him. Without any hesitation I reached over and put my hand upon him and said, "You dumb spirit, come out!" As I did, I commanded, "Speak to your mother!" He turned to his mother and spoke for the first time in over three months. Then he talked to all of us. God had set him free from this evil thing that had attached itself to him.

I did not go looking for problems or for people oppressed of the devil, but as God brought me into their pathway I was not afraid to assist and pray for the afflicted.

5.   THE "FATHER DIVINE" SPIRIT

I found a strange incident of demon oppression in Indianapolis, Indiana. The pastor asked if I would go and pray for one of the families of the church as the mother was ill. I went to the home where a mother and daughter lived together, but found I could not pray. I knelt down to pray for her but I could not close my eyes.

I said, "There is something strange in this house."

The mother said, "Well, what could it be?"

I said, "I don't know!" I walked around the room for a little bit. The daughter and the mother watched me. I noticed a pile of magazines and reached down to pick one up and found Father Divine's magazine from New York. I said, "What is this doing here?"

The daughter said, "I have just returned from Father Divine's heaven and I saw the mighty miracles that he performs and I communicate with him by spirit."

I looked at her and said, "You have received the spirit of that man, which is the devil, and you have received it within you as a spirit of sorcery. You are in communication with evil spirits and I cannot pray for your mother until you get rid of these things."

Here was a high school teacher who had given herself over to evil spirits. They had attached themselves to her mother and now she was desperately sick. The doctors could find nothing wrong with her. It was this spirit tormenting them in the home.

The woman became willing for us to pray and we exorcised those spirits from that mother and from that home in Jesus' name.

From these early experiences I have gone on to deal with many hundreds of cases of demon oppression and possession in this country and in other countries. In fact, almost every day I am called upon to pray for those needing deliverance by telephone or in person.

6. CLARITA VILLANUEVA—MANILA, PHILIPPINES

A notable deliverance known around the world was in Bilibid Prison in the Philippines when the Lord set Clarita Villanueva free from demon power. Something unseen by natural eyes would bite her. This went on for some three weeks.

The Lord spoke to me and said He would heal her if I would go and pray for her. I did go and the Lord set her free and through this miracle a great revival came to the nation of the Philippines and to the city of Manila. The mayor of the city, who had seen her afflicted state, was so moved that he offered us the Roxas Park in front of the city hall for a crusade. There, in six weeks of great meetings, thousands of people made decisions to follow and serve the Lord Jesus Christ. The people came from the entire region of the Philippines and went back into their own towns and cities glorifying God for what had happened. The healing of this girl in the Philippines caused the religious complexion of the nation to change. Churches that had a most difficult time getting members became full of people. Many denominations received blessings because of the revival that God gave through the healing of this girl.

7. THE INVISIBLE BOY

Another tremendous deliverance by God's power was with the boy in the Philippines who would disappear. He would just simply evaporate into thin air. He would disappear from his schoolroom causing great consternation. The teacher had a nervous breakdown and never taught again.

The members of his family were near a nervous breakdown. They were Roman Catholic people and did not know what to do. They were trying to safeguard themselves against the publicity by not getting this thing in the newspaper. Otherwise, they would be hounded to death by the public. This had gone on for a year when a Methodist minister found them and brought them to my meetings where God healed that boy instantly. We cast that spirit out of him in the name of Jesus Christ, and he was set free and is still free.

8. THE FUTURE

The Lord has revealed to me that there will be millions of people in the world who will need deliverance from evil spirits in the days ahead of us.

Occultism, witchcraft, fortune telling, astrology, and spiritism will greatly increase. Many books are now in print on the New Age Movement.

The church must prepare itself for the greatest battle of the ages in the realm of the spirit world. The Bible prophesies a coming time of incomprehensible chaos with a tribulation period of incalculable proportions. It will be a savage time of world woe masterminded by Satan and his hosts.

Many ministers must be trained and taught the great apostolic truths. In our Indiana Christian University we instruct students to exorcise spirits by faith in God. Jesus said in John 8:36, *If the Son therefore shall make you free, ye shall be free indeed.*

INDIANA CHRISTIAN UNIVERSITY

DEMONOLOGY & DELIVERANCE I

Lesson 21

SEVEN STEPS TOWARD DEMON POSSESSION PART I

INTRODUCTION:

The subject of demon power is not spoken of in many religious circles these days. Many simply don't believe in demons. The subject is taboo (I have noticed that the less the church says about demons and the less we expose them, the more control they assume over human destiny.) It is only when we pull the drapes back and expose demon power that we can set people free.

Christians have been taught to fear the devil. I don't understand how modern Christians became cowards. Even some preachers are afraid of Satan.

The Bible does not teach us to fear the devil, but to resist him. Jesus Christ didn't say we should run from Satan. Instead, the Great Commission says that those who have faith shall cast out devils.

Christians possess authority from Jesus Christ to exorcise evil spirits. We have no reason whatsoever to be afraid of them.

READING:

Ephesians 6:11-13, *Finally, my brethren, be strong in the Lord, and in the power of his might.*
v. 12, *For we wrestle not against flesh and blood, but against principalities, against powers, against the rulers of the darkness of this world, against spiritual wickedness in high places.*
v. 13, *Wherefore take unto you the whole armour of God, that ye may be able to withstand in the evil day, and having done all, to stand.*

In this passage of scripture, the Apostle Paul is teaching that our warfare is not in the flesh. We are not to fight men and women, we are to fight the powers of darkness of this world.

Paul also said in 2 Corinthians 10:3-5, *For though we walk in the flesh, we do not war after the flesh:*
v. 4, *For the weapons of our warfare are not carnal, but mighty through God to the pulling down of strong holds;*
v. 5, *Casting down imaginations, and every high thing that exalteth itself against the knowledge of God, and bringing into captivity every thought to the obedience of Christ.*

SEVEN STEPS SATAN USES TO TAKE OVER AN IMMORTAL SOUL

1. **Regression:** Reversion to earlier behavior patterns; to go backward

2. **Repression:** To restrain; to squeeze; to prevent natural expression; to keep down; to hold back

3. **Suppression:** To press under; to keep back; to conceal; to exclude desire and feeling

4. **Depression:** Low spirits; gloominess; dejection; sadness; a decrease in force or activity; an emotional condition, either neurotic or psychotic, characterized by feelings of hopelessness or inadequacy

5. **Oppression:** Pressure to crush; to smother; to overpower or overwhelm; to harass; to ravish, or to rape

6. **Obsession:** To besiege; to haunt as of evil spirits; to be fixed on a single idea to an unreasonable degree

7. **Possession:** To inhabit; to occupy; to control; to hold as a property; to dominate; to actuate; to rule by extraneous forces

I do not mean to suggest that in every case of demon assault these seven steps, or stages, will be readily evident. It might well be that there are some intermediary steps not discussed in this study guide.

Perhaps in some cases it may even appear that the steps occur in a different order from the progression outlined here. However, based on my experience and study, I believe that most people who become demon possessed travel down this ruinous road, taking these seven terrible steps toward complete domination by Satan's power.

Let me stress that the devil seldom takes a life all at once. He does it a little at a time, step by step. Sometimes he is able to assume complete control rapidly, but most often it is a slow process over a period of weeks, months, or even years.

1. REGRESSION

I call the first step, when the devil attacks a human personality, regression. It is a human battle against his God-given abilities of release and expression.

To regress in the human personality is to go backward in spiritual force and power. The human person is built for progress, advancement, and understanding. When this goes into reverse, it is the first warning that negative powers are evident.

This can be resisted and overcome by prayer and praise unto the Lord. *Key*

2. REPRESSION

A.   The second of the seven steps toward demon possession is repression.

It is most interesting to me that God makes every human an expressionist. The moment a baby is born, the doctor spanks it. He wants expression. If he doesn't get it he pronounces the baby dead!

God desires exuberant expression from us. He wants our eyes to talk and our faces to light up. He made us to express something. Anyone who represses that function is doing the work of the devil. God is the Great Expression. In the Bible, anytime a prophet or apostle looked into heaven there was a great movement with singing and praising God.

God wants human expression. The devil doesn't. The devil is wicked and miserable with no joy. He knows no happiness and no expression of peace.

Therefore, to repress a person is to destroy the natural expression which God gave him when he was born. To repress a person is to restrain from without. To repress a personality takes away the joy and gladness of that life. God did not create human lives to be restrained by abnormal environment.

NOTES

STUDY GUIDE

INDIANA CHRISTIAN UNIVERSITY

DEMONOLOGY & DELIVERANCE I

Lesson 22

SEVEN STEPS TOWARD DEMON POSSESSION PART II

2. REPRESSION: (continued)

B. Repressive Religion

You may be surprised to learn that repression is often found in churches and religions. People go to church and never experience the joy of salvation. For example, a man goes to worship service and takes with him a little boy or girl. They walk along the sidewalk chatting and laughing. Within fifty steps of the church suddenly something happens to the man. His eyes go into a fixed glare. His body becomes as rigid as a board. He walks softly into the church, finds his pew, and sits down. For the next hour he sits there like a mummy, with no expression of any kind. When the meeting is over he gets up and goes out. As he gets about fifty steps away from the church, he sighs and says, "I'm glad that's over for another week."

Some church members go to church as though it were a funeral parlor. If God did manifest Himself in any manner, it would scare them to death. According to the Bible, real worship is different. When Israel dedicated Solomon's Temple, there were musical instruments played and praises sung to God.

1 Kings 8:65-66, *And at that time Solomon held a feast, and all Israel with him, a great congregation, from the entering in of Hamath unto the river of Egypt, before the LORD our God, seven days and seven days, even fourteen days.*
v. 66, *On the eighth day he sent the people away: and they blessed the king, and went unto their tents joyful and glad of heart for all the goodness that the LORD had done for David his servant, and for Israel his people.*

II Chronicles 7:8-10, *Also at the same time Solomon kept the feast seven days, and all Israel with him, a very great congregation, from the entering in of Hamath unto the river of Egypt.*
v. 9, *And in the eighth day they made a solemn assembly: for they kept the dedication of the altar seven days, and the feast seven days.*
v. 10, *And on the three and twentieth day of the seventh month he sent the people away into their tents, glad and merry in heart for the goodness that the LORD had shewed unto David, and to Solomon, and to Israel his people.*

Today, much religion lacks expression of the spirit and soul of man. Instead, it represses and drives back inside fervent feelings toward God. In my services, we sing joyful choruses because God's joy comes to us from expressing ourselves.

When the devil destroys a life, one step is the repressing of natural joys.

S
C. Repressive Homes and People

Often, repression begins at home. Every home should take a survey of its members. The daughter in the home can be the repressor. When something goes wrong she flies into a tantrum, and it takes everybody in the house to get things back to normal again. Sometimes it can be a wife and mother who causes everybody to tiptoe around. If something displeases her she makes the home a miserable place to live. It also can be a belligerent husband. The family can be happy and smiling until he opens the door. Then you would think death had walked in. He bellows and yells until everybody just dies inside. That man represses what could be a happy home.

Further, repression can happen at work. A foreman, if he likes, can be "as mean as the devil" to the men who work for him. He can curse and scream at the men until they are nervous wrecks. Finally, the men even hate to go to work. When they do, they won't smile, and they will barely speak when the foreman is around. They become repressed.

You ask, "But what has this to do with the devil?" It is the devil who makes people act like this. Satan wants to steal all the joy and happiness from every human. Repression becomes an open door for further works of the devil.

It is a bad sign when a person goes silent. A soul in solitude is headed for trouble. Eyes that gaze in a fixed stare reveal bondage. To lose the good spirit of joy and happiness is to take the road to a ruined personality. One who represses all his inner feelings becomes a walking dead man.

Every Christian should be careful not to repress others. Let every human express himself joyfully.

3. SUPPRESSION

As the dictionary defines "suppress," it means to abnormally squeeze down. It also means to conceal, to suppress information.

Feelings and desires when not expressed can be suppressed or kept back.

The devil is very keen on suppression. It represents another step toward the deterioration of emotion and the destruction of full and complete personal happiness.

Suppression is an artificial thing which comes from without. It is an unholy action because God and the entire Bible reveal dynamic expression, openness of desire, and exuberance of feeling.

Let us realize that the devil causes regression of the spiritual life. This is reversion to earlier behavior patterns, especially with the emotions and expressions.

Then Satan moves to repression which is a great step downward. It has to do with restraining or holding back the natural expressions of life.

With suppression we have concealment or greater pressures moving against the victorious Christian life.

Please note that the devil will not stop at the third step, or any other place. However, you can stop him and refuse to be regressed, repressed, or suppressed.

4. DEPRESSION

A. The fourth step toward complete demon domination is depression. This is a big step down the path toward complete satanic control of a personality.

In depression, there is a broken spirit. One is pressed down until his spirit is crushed. To remain depressed for a long period of time is of the devil. It is not normal to life. God doesn't want anyone depressed and sad. Any person who stays depressed for an extended time is sick. The devil takes advantage of people in that state of mind and moves in with conflict and confusions that will destroy their happiness, their homes, and their businesses. Depression will destroy every part of their natural lives.

It is a sad thing to observe the masses of people in America today who are depressed. Personally, I refuse to be depressed by the devil or anybody else! God does not depress mankind. The devil is the depressor of human life.

By experience I have discovered that a downcast face and sad soul won't help resolve problems. They won't pay bills! They do no good at all.

Psalm 42:5, *Why art thou cast down, O my soul? and why art thou disquieted in me? hope thou in God: for I shall yet praise him for the help of his countenance.*

King David in Psalm 103:1 says, *Bless the Lord, O my soul: and all that is within me, bless his holy name.*

That's the way you should get up every morning! Start the day blessing the Lord.

B.   Causes of depression

There are some people who are religiously depressed. They think there is great holiness in a long face. I want to assure you there is no biblical basis for this idea.

Traditions can produce depression. I met a Christian woman who was deeply depressed. The pastor said she had lost her husband about six months before. He had been a fine Christian businessman, and she was a very capable businesswoman on her own. Financially, she had no problems, but following religious tradition, she dressed in black from head to toe. Every day for more than six months she had been in mourning. I saw that she carried a burden of depression.

I asked her, "Why are you wearing black?"

"Oh, I'm in mourning for my dead husband." she said.

"Was he a sinner?" I questioned.

"Oh, no!" she exclaimed.

"Then why do you look so sad about his going to heaven?" I asked. This was the first time anyone had spoken the truth as to her melancholy. I asked if she thought they wore black in heaven.

She replied, "No, I think they wear white up there."

"Then if your husband is in heaven where there is life, why don't you dress cheerfully? If he could see your sad face and those mournful clothes, it would make him sad even in heaven."

Why did I talk to this lady so plainly? She was going downhill. She was fast becoming a recluse. She felt that if she smiled or laughed it would be disrespectful to her husband up in heaven.

I want you to know that in the next service she came dressed in white from veil to shoes. I looked at her and said "Well, something must have happened."

She told me, "Yes, I want to look like my husband, dressed in white!" That woman became one of the most inspiring Christians in the community.

110

She now works in her church and leads a victorious Christian life. The devil was simply destroying her Christian witness with depression.

Tradition often demands a long face and a sad countenance. God says in Proverbs 17:22, *A merry heart doeth good like medicine.*

It is a terrible situation when millions of people are deeply depressed. If God does not send one of His servants to set them free, they will slip deeper into demon domination.

Depression is often triggered by loss or deep trouble. Heavy financial burdens, family problems, or disappointment can depress a person leaving them dejected and forlorn.

Depression is dangerous because it often brings about an abnormal state of inactivity. The person may sit staring into space, hearing nothing, saying nothing, and doing nothing. Inside, he feels sadness too deep to express and too painful for tears. He has reached the point where he sees no need to even try any longer.

Almost everyone has feelings of depression now and then. Usually, the average person overcomes it after a few hours, or at most a day or two. A word of comfort or encouragement from a friend, a passage from God's Word, a good night's rest, or a change of scenery is enough to bring new hope and renewed strength to begin living again. If depression and melancholy hang on, then the victim may be headed for serious trouble.

The devil would like every Christian in the world to be depressed. He knows that depressed people are not energetic or enthusiastic about anything. A depressed person becomes listless, inactive, and disinterested in what goes on around him. If enough Christians were depressed, Satan would have free rule in the world. He would have no one to oppose him and thwart his evil plans to control the world and its people.

5. OPPRESSION

A.   The fifth stage through which the devil drags a person to destroy and possess him is what I call oppression. It is a vast area of human experience far deeper and more involved than depression.

To oppress anyone is to weigh him down with something he is not able to carry. The children of Israel were oppressed in Egypt. They were cruelly treated, beaten unmercifully, and crushed down until they couldn't carry their burdens any longer. If you are oppressed, you are burdened with a load that is more than you can carry.

111

B. Oppression through disease

Acts 10:38, . . .*God anointed Jesus of Nazareth with the Holy Ghost and with power: who went about doing good, and healing all that were oppressed of the devil; for God was with him.*

This passage tells us that God the Father sent Jesus to this earth to heal all those who were oppressed of the devil. Christ came especially to heal the oppressed of the devil. This suggests that oppression can be in the realm of disease. In America, millions are so oppressed. I do not believe disease is natural anymore than a beautiful tree would be natural with every kind of bug and disease covering its branches. I believe that it is natural to be healthy, and that it is unnatural to be unhealthy. I believe that disease comes because the devil is trying to make everyone he can sick. If every man in the world were a doctor, every woman were a nurse, and every house were a hospital, there would still be millions of sick people.

C. Oppression through fear

One of the greatest causes of oppression is fear. Millions of people are oppressed by fear. There are people who worry all the time about going out of their minds. That's what the devil wants them to do. God's Word declares that the devil is a liar and the father of lies.

John 8:44, *Ye are of your father the devil, and the lusts of your father ye will do. He was a murderer from the begining, and abode not in the truth, because there is no truth in him. When he speaketh a lie, he speaketh of his own: for he is a liar, and the father of it.*

The devil wants to torment people. He wants to hurt them. He wants to mock and laugh at God while he does it. God's people do not have to suffer this terrible fear. One of the great blessings of Christianity is a strong mind which is able to reject the unreasonable demands of fear.

D. Ways and means of oppression

Satan may use many means to try to destroy you by oppression. He may try to crush your spirit by having people you thought were your friends attack you viciously. He may seek to trample you down through disaster and woes. He may try to overpower you with a great display of demonic power which hurts you on all sides until you feel helpless against his cruel onslaught. He might weigh you down with an awesome sense of responsibility for all the people and actions in your family or community. He might even burden you with a feeling that all your trouble and misfortune is punishment from God for some great sin. All these things fall into the category of demonic oppression.

E.   Oppression can be defeated

Exercise your Christian dominion over the devil's power. You do this through faith, prayer, and action. Have faith to command God's power in your life. Pray to strengthen your inner being. Act to overcome and destroy the works of the devil.

If you are oppressed of the devil with disease, with fear, with nervousness, with anything--receive deliverance now!

6.   OBSESSION

The sixth way the devil can take over a human life is by means of obsession.

A.   Two kinds of obsession

As with most things, there are two kinds of obsession. One we could call positive obsession. For example, Christ was obsessed with His own destiny of saving the world. The Apostle Paul was obsessed with the gospel of Jesus Christ so much that a Roman governor told him he was a mad man. These were magnificent obsessions. In this study we are dealing with a negative obsession which destroys the human personality. *good Kinds*

B.   You can't save yourself.

At this stage of demon domination, I doubt that the individual being hurt by Satan could save himself without the assistance of another. I feel sure that a person who is repressed can shake it off in Jesus' name and be free. I believe that a person who is depressed, when reminded of the danger, can rid himself of it and have a happy, joyful spirit. It is possible for one who is oppressed to help himself. When we get to this stage where obsession has assumed control of a person's thinking, he needs outside help to be set free. The reason for this is that when one has an obsession, the mind is changed. Black becomes white and white seems black. A straight thing is now crooked and a lie becomes the truth. This loss of perspective causes the person to be out of step with everyone else around him, he does not realize that he is obsessed with some wicked thing.

C.   What is obsession?

By definition, it is an evil spirit's deceiving a person and impelling him to unreasonable action. The dictionary says that it is a persistent and inescapable preoccupation with an idea or emotion. This idea usually has no relationship with reality.

113

D. Causes of obsession

1) Obsession can come by believing a lie. If what we believe is out of line with what others believe, we should check our beliefs and seek to know the truth. Otherwise, the devil may deceive us with an evil obsession.

2) Obsession can come through jealousy. A husband or wife may get an idea that his/her spouse is not loyal. This thing preys upon his/her mind. The devil makes the idea take root and grow like an evil vine. Finally, every time the mate turns his back, the jealous one says, "Now he has done something wrong." Their very lives are destroyed simply because of the evilness of jealousy.

3) Hatred can be an avenue to obsession. One can believe that others dislike him and begin to hate them until he can't think straight. He can't see what is true because hatred has blinded him. This hatred becomes an obsession.

4) Certain sins, such as moral transgressions, can become an obsession. One may become overwhelmed by his immorality to the point that he is unable to see anything pure and holy because he is blinded with this obsession.

E. Protect your willpower.

1) The devil has many avenues by which to invade the human personality. When anyone develops a complex in any form, that person should pray, read the Word of God, and consult with a minister or brother or sister in Christ who has spiritual discernment to see if the devil is trying to obsess his entire being. An obsessed person comes to the place where he has no willpower. He had no strength to resist, so he becomes a slave. His mind gets on one track and it is impossible to change his thinking.

2) Willpower is one of the greatest gifts God has given us. We should never lend our willpower to anyone. One of the great dangers of hypnotism, for instance, is that one must yield his mind and spirit to another individual who may be utterly unscrupulous. There is danger that one may become a slave to hypnotism. As a result of being hypnotized frequently, one could become a servant to the one who places him in the trance. I warn everyone never to submit to hypnotism in any form.

3) I feel the same way about fortune-telling. It can control a person's thinking until he tries to shape his life to fit the random predictions of a fraudulent seer. I also feel very strongly about astrology, which can grip a person until he must read each day to see if the stars are right for him.

4) Of course, drug and alcohol addiction can obsess a life until a person is not able to govern himself anymore. Often it seems that alcoholism is a spirit.

Although a person says that he will never touch alcohol again, he suddenly has no power to resist it when this thing comes upon him. The same is true with certain drugs which a person should resist as strongly as possible.

5) Anything that can destroy your willpower should be avoided. God wants His children to be men and women of decision who know right from wrong. They must let no obsession take over the mastery of their soul.

F. Overcoming obsession

Once a person has fallen prey to demonic obsession, he needs a man or woman of God to pray a prayer of deliverance over him in order to be free.

Do not feel that it is difficult or impossible to be set free from demon obsession. Jesus can set you free. He wants to set you free. He has the power to set you free. Do not be afraid of the devil's power. Only believe, because Jesus said in Mark 9:23, . . . *If thou canst believe, all things are possible to them that believeth.*

7. POSSESSION

Demon possession is the final step by which the devil captures an immortal soul. In this area we seek to be very cautious and conservative in our thinking.

A. The step from obsession to possession is a long step. The devil would like to push every obsessed person fully and finally into his clutches of full possession. For up to this stage, a person is not truly possessed.

I do not find many people in this final stage, although there are hundreds in the other stages.

The demon-possessed person is under the absolute, total, and complete jurisdiction of the devil. He has no mind of his own. The ownership of his soul by the devil is complete. Satan is now the master of all that person's thinking and actions. He has full control of that life. The person has no mind to think, no spirit to reach for God, and no soul to pray for help! He is helpless in the hands of a diabolical monster.

B. Discerning demonic power

How can we know when a person is demon possessed? There are many ways.

1) I have observed in dealing with demon-possessed people that often the devil uses their voices and throats to speak. For example, I have heard men under the influence of demon power speak to me with the voices of women. I have also heard women with the gruff voices of men coming out of their throats. An evil spirit is speaking through them.

115

A strange example of this phenomenon was the case of the girl in the Philippines who was bitten by devils. She cursed God, Jesus Christ, the Holy Spirit, the blood of Jesus, and me in English. After she was healed, we discovered that she could barely speak a word of English. Therefore, the devil was using her mouth, lips, and throat to blaspheme God.

2)   Demon possession reveals itself sometimes in forms of insanity, both temporary and complete. Doctors who work in institutions and asylums know that a patient's mind may be very clear at one time and that at another time the person may become like an animal. This is the coming and going of demon power within the person. These people who are lost in a world of gloom and darkness and misery have the saddest faces in the world. They have lost the power to rise above their problems. The devil has actually captured them and they live in Satan's chains.

3)   Demon possession is always reflected in the eyes. The personality is projected through the eyes. A demon-possessed person's eyes are not normal. He cannot hold up his head to you. The devil will not let him. If he does, his eyes focus in a demonic glare. The devil changes the windows of the soul when he moves in.

Matthew 6:22-23, *The light of the body is the eye: if therefore thine eye be single, thy whole body shall be full of light.*
v. 23, *But if thine eye be evil, thy whole body shall be full of darkness. If therefore the light that is in thee be darkness, how great is that darkness!*

4)   Often, the way a person walks reveals demon possession. The devil takes over his body and he cannot walk as other people do. There is a strangeness in the way he walks.

5)   For God's servant, the way to tell if a person is demon possessed is spiritual discernment. If God is within me and the devil is within another person, when we meet there is a tremendous clash of spirits inside. Some would call it a conflict of personalities, but it is not. It has nothing to do with personality. It is the warfare of opposite spirits.

6)   Demon power is "catching." The devil's power is as contagious as the measles. Those under his power want others under it too. A smoker tries to spread his habit to a non-smoker, a dope addict deceives others until they are "hooked," leprous immoral perverts look for the unwary to lead them into sin, latent victims are urged into the trap by aggressors, and people with fear and depression may have an unreasonable desire that others suffer as they do. The first stages of demon possession often result from association with others already under the devil's control.

116

To some people, the words "demon possession" mean something dirty. We need to have a new approach to this subject. Some of the finest people in the world have been assaulted by the devil and, in some instances, conquered. They need the help of Christ and the church right now. The Lord is just as willing to heal a person who is tormented by the devil as He is to heal a bad cold. Deliverance comes through the same kind of power with the same anointing and the same kind of faith.

C. Don't fear the devil.

In the last days every believer and disciple of Christ should set men free from the devil's power. Many Christians do not realize the authority and power which belongs to them as children of God. The Bible says in James 4:7, *Resist the devil and he will flee from you.* He runs from us! There is no point in both of us running.

The Holy Spirit resolves all problems. The church is commissioned to cast out devils. We must fulfill The Great Commission (Mark 16:17).

I believe it is now time for a great freedom to be set in motion. Men and women of courage should set out to bring freedom to those who are repressed, depressed, suppressed, oppressed, obsessed, and possessed by the devil's power. The same Christ who set the prisoners free two thousand years ago can set them free today.

1 John 3:8, *He that committeth sin is of the devil; for the devil sinneth from the beginning. For this purpose the Son of God was manifested, that he might destroy the works of the devil.*

There is something you must know if Satan has attacked you. You are not a prisoner without hope. You can be set free. Have faith in God. Believe and you shall be free by His mighty power.

NOTES

INDIANA CHRISTIAN UNIVERSITY

DEMONOLOGY & DELIVERANCE I

Lesson 23

COMMUNICATION WITH DEVILS FORBIDDEN BY DIVINE DECREE

INTRODUCTION:

A. Demon power has to do with the worship of other gods.

B. The origin of all problems was when Lucifer the fallen angel said, *I will exalt my throne* . . . (Isaiah 14:13). He desired worship. He caused rebellion in heaven.

C. This same Satan deceived Eve in the Garden of Eden and caused Adam and Eve to be expelled (Genesis 3).

D. Through the centuries Satan has sought to be worshipped.

God has spoken clearly and specifically about the matter.

1. LEVITICUS 19:31, *Regard not them that have familiar spirits, neither seek after wizards, to be defiled by them: I am the LORD your God.*

2. LEVITICUS 20:6, *And the soul that turneth after such as have familiar spirits, and after wizards, to go a-whoring after them, I will even set my face against that soul, and will cut him off from among his people.*

3. DEUTERONOMY 18:10, *There shall not be found among you any one that maketh his son or his daughter to pass through the fire, or that useth divination, or an observer of times, or an enchanter, or a witch.*

4. ISAIAH 8:19-21, *And when they shall say unto you, Seek unto them that have familiar spirits, and unto wizards that peep, and that mutter: should not a people seek unto their God? for the living to the dead?*

v. 20, *To the law and to the testimony: if they speak not according to this word, it is because there is no light in them.*

v. 21, *And they shall pass through it, hardly bestead and hungry: and it shall come to pass, that when they shall be hungry, they shall fret themselves, and curse their king and their God, and look upward.*

5.   1 CHRONICLES 10:13-14, *So Saul died for his transgression which he committed against the LORD, even against the word of the LORD, which he kept not, and also for asking counsel of one that had a familiar spirit, to inquire of it;*

v. 14, *And inquired not of the LORD: therefore he slew him, and turned the kingdom unto David the son of Jesse.*

6.   LUKE 4:41, *And devils also came out of many, crying out, and saying, Thou art Christ the Son of God. And he rebuking them suffered them not to speak: for they knew that he was Christ.*

7.   ACTS 16:16, *And it came to pass, as we went to prayer, a certain damsel possessed with a spirit of divination met us, which brought her masters much gain by soothsaying.*

8.   1 TIMOTHY 4:1, *Now the Spirit speaketh expressly, that in the latter times some shall depart from the faith, giving heed to seducing spirits, and doctrines of devils.*

9.   2 PETER 2:1-3, *But there were false prophets also among the people, even as there shall be false teachers among you, who privily shall bring in damnable heresies, even denying the Lord that bought them, and bring upon themselves swift destruction.*

v. 2, *And many shall follow their pernicious ways; by reason of whom the way of truth shall be evil spoken of.*

v. 3, *And through covetousness shall they with feigned words make merchandise of you: whose judgment now of a long time lingereth not, and their damnation slumbereth not.*

10. 1 JOHN 4:1-6, *Beloved, believe not every spirit, but try the spirits whether they are of God: because many false prophets are gone out into the world.*
v. 2, Hereby know ye the Spirit of God: Every spirit that confesseth that Jesus Christ is come in the flesh is of God:
v. 3, And every spirit that confesseth not that Jesus is come in the flesh is not of God: and this is that spirit of antichrist, whereof ye have heard that it should come; and even now already is it in the world.
v. 4, Ye are of God, little children, and have overcome them: because greater is he that is in you, than he that is in the world.
v. 5, They are of the world: therefore speak they of the world, and the world heareth them.
v. 6, We are of God: he that knoweth God heareth us; he that is not of God heareth not us. Hereby know we the spirit of truth, and the spirit of error.

NOTES

_____

_____

_____

_____

_____

_____

_____

_____

_____

_____

_____

_____

_____

_____

_____

_____

_____

_____

_____

_____

_____

_____

DEMONOLOGY & DELIVERANCE I

Lesson 24

THE CHURCH REPLACES LUCIFER AND HIS HOST BEFORE THE THRONE OF GOD

INTRODUCTION:

In heaven, God created three angels who, in particular, were to govern and administer His will. They carried out His desires to the angelic citizens of heaven and to special persons here on earth.

A.   THE ANGEL GABRIEL

Gabriel is God's messenger and minister. We can deduce that he leads one-third of the angels of heaven.

Daniel 9:21-22, *While I was still in prayer, Gabriel, the man I had seen in the earlier vision, came to me in swift flight about the time of the evening sacrifice.*
v. 22, *He instructed me and said to me, "Daniel, I have now come to give you insight and understanding* (NIV).

Daniel 8:16, *And I heard a man's voice from the Ulai, who called, and said, "Gabriel, tell this man the meaning of the vision"* (NIV).

We link Gabriel to the Christmas story. We remember him as the angelic messenger who appeared to Zacharias, the priest, telling him his prayer was answered and his wife Elizabeth would bear a son and that his name would be John (Luke 1:11-19).

We next meet Gabriel announcing to the young virgin, Mary, that she would bring forth a son and that His name would be Jesus (Luke 1:27-32).

B.   THE ANGEL MICHAEL

Michael is God's warrior. In the Bible he defended God's people. We meet Michael when he appeared to help Daniel.

Daniel 10:13, *But the prince of the kingdom of Persia withstood me one and twenty days: but lo, Michael, one of the chief princes, came to help me; and I remained there with the kings of Persia.*

Michael spoke words of comfort to Daniel, thereby imparting strength and peace (v. 16-18). Whenever we encounter Michael, it is in connection with some type of spiritual struggle.

In addition to Old Testament references, we encounter Michael in the New Testament book of Jude and in the book of Revelation where he is depicted as contending with Lucifer and his angels (Revelation 12:7-9).

C.   THE ANGEL LUCIFER

Lucifer was the covering angel who led praise and worship before the throne.

Ezekiel 28:13-14, *Thou hast been in Eden the garden of God; every precious stone was thy covering, the sardius, topaz, and the diamond, the beryl, the onyx, and the jasper, the sapphire, the emerald, and the carbuncle, and gold: the workmanship of thy tabrets and of thy pipes was prepared in thee in the day that thou wast created.*
v. 14, *Thou art the anointed cherub that covereth; and I have set thee so: thou wast upon the holy mountain of God; thou hast walked up and down in the midst of the stones of fire.*

Lucifer was a perfect angel called "son of the morning." He mounted a rebellion in heaven and fell.

1)   Lucifer removed from heaven

When Lucifer, because of rebellion, was removed from heaven with the host of angels who followed him, there was left a great vacancy. This emptiness was before the throne of God.

Isaiah 14:12-15, *How art thou fallen from heaven, O Lucifer, son of the morning! how art thou cut down to the ground, which didst weaken the nations!*
v. 13, *For thou hast said in thine heart, I will ascend into heaven, I will exalt my throne above the stars of God: I will sit also upon the mount of the congregation, in the sides of the north:*
v. 14, *I will ascend above the heights of the clouds; I will be like the most High.*
v. 15, *Yet thou shalt be brought down to hell, to the sides of the pit.*

1. JESUS CAME TO EARTH

In the council chambers of the divine Trinity it was decided that Jesus would come to earth and purchase with His blood a host of redeemed, rejoicing saints to stand before the throne of God and replace the angel and his hosts who had been removed.

Ephesians 1:4-7, *According as he hath chosen us in him before the foundation of the world, that we should be holy and without blame before him in love:*
v. 5, Having predestinated us unto the adoption of children by Jesus Christ to himself, according to the good pleasure of his will,
v. 6, To the praise of the glory of his grace, wherein he hath made us accepted in the beloved.
v. 7, In whom we have redemption through his blood, the forgiveness of sins, according to the riches of his grace.

Ephesians 1:11-12, *In whom also we have obtained an inheritance, being predestinated according to the purpose of him who worketh all things after the counsel of his own will.*
v. 12, That we should be to the praise of his glory, who first trusted in Christ.

Hebrews 1:1-8, *God, who at sundry times and in divers manners spake in time past unto the fathers by the prophets,*
v. 2, Hath in these last days spoken unto us by his Son, whom he hath appointed heir of all things, by whom also he made the worlds;
v. 3, Who being the brightness of his glory, and the express image of his person, and upholding all things by the word of his power, when he had by himself purged our sins, sat down on the right hand of the Majesty on high;
v. 4, Being made so much better than the angels, as he hath by inheritance obtained a more excellent name than they.
v. 5, For unto which of the angels said he at any time, Thou art my Son, this day have I begotten thee? And again, I will be to him a Father, and he shall be to me a Son?
v. 6, And again, when he bringeth in the first begotten into the world, he saith, And let all the angels of God worship him.
v. 7, And of the angels he saith, Who maketh his angels spirits, and his ministers a flame of fire.
v. 8, But unto the Son he saith, Thy throne, O God, is for ever and ever: a sceptre of righteousness is the sceptre of thy kingdom.

2. SECOND COMING

With the Second Coming of Christ and the gathering of all the redeemed of all ages, heaven will again be filled. The book of Revelation speaks over and over again of the heavenly multitude's shouting, praising, and worshipping God.

Revelation 19:1, *And after these things I heard a great voice of much people in heaven, saying, Alleluia; Salvation, and glory, and honour, and power, unto the Lord our God.*

In heaven we will meet Gabriel and his messengers. We will be with Michael and his warriors.

Before the throne of God will be the redeemed; and, if our names have been written in the Lamb's book of life, we will be among that great throng.

In speaking of the New Jerusalem, the Bible says in Revelation 21:24a, 27, *And the nations of them which are saved shall walk in the light of it. . .And there shall in no wise enter into it anything that defileth. . .but they which are written in the Lamb's book of life.*

Revelation 19:5-7, *And a voice came out of the throne, saying, Praise our God, all ye his servants, and ye that fear him, both small and great.*
v. 6, *And I heard as it were the voice of a great multitude, and as the voice of many waters, and as the voice of mighty thunderings, saying, Alleluia: for the Lord God omnipotent reigneth.*
v. 7, *Let us be glad and rejoice, and give honour to him: for the marriage of the Lamb is come, and his wife hath made herself ready.*

3. LUCIFER THE REVOLUTIONARY

Lucifer and his angels or demons will be forever doomed in the lake of fire mentioned five times in the book of Revelation.

Revelation 20:10, *And the devil that deceived them was cast into the lake of fire and brimstone, where the beast and the false prophet are, and shall be tormented day and night for ever and ever.*

4. THE ETERNAL AGES WILL RESUME

Revelation 21:1-3, *And I saw a new heaven and a new earth: for the first heaven and the first earth were passed away; and there was no more sea.*
v. 2, *And I John saw the holy city, new Jerusalem, coming down from God out of heaven, prepared as a bride adorned for her husband.*
v. 3, *And I heard a great voice out of heaven saying, Behold, the tabernacle of God is with men, and he will dwell with them, and they shall be his people, and God himself shall be with them, and be their God.*

5. YOU AND I WILL BE A PART OF IT

Revelation 21:7, *He that overcometh shall inherit all things; and I will be his God, and he shall be my son.*

DEMONOLOGY & DELIVERANCE I

Lesson 25

QUESTIONS AND ANSWERS REGARDING DEMON POWER

1. DID THE EARLY CHURCH FATHERS BELIEVE IN OR TEACH EXORCISM FROM DEMON POWER?

There is recorded history to support a positive response to this question. During the first centuries of the Christian Church, the spiritual leaders dealt extensively with demon power. Here are some examples:

Justin Martyr, in his *Apology LIV*, insisted that heathen mythology was originated by demon power:

> "The evil spirits were not satisfied with saying before Christ's appearance that those who were said to be sons of Jupiter were born of him: but after He had appeared and had been born among men, and when they learned how He had been foretold by the prophets and knew He should be believed upon and looked for in every nation, they again put forward other men, the Samaritans, Simon and Menander, who did mighty works by magic and deceived many and still kept them deceived."

From this quotation we see that Justin Martyr had a real grip on the functioning of demon power.

The Church father, Lactantius, in his *Divine Institutes, Number 2*, says:

> "The inventors of astrology, and soothsaying, and divination, and those productions which are called oracles, and necromancy, and the art of magic, and whatever evil practices besides these men exercise, either openly or in secret: these are they who taught men from the worship of the true

God, caused the countenances of dead kings to be erected and consecrated, and assumed to themselves their names."

The great Church father, Augustine, wrote in chapter 25 of his *City of God, Book 2*:

"What spirit can that be which by a hidden inspiration stirs men's corruption, and goads them into adultery, and feeds on full-fledged iniquity, unless it be the same that finds pleasure in such religious ceremonies, sets in the temples images of devils, and loves to see in play the images of vices; that whispers in secret some righteous saying to deceive the few who are good, and scatters in public invitations to profligacy, to gain possession of millions who are wicked?"

In chapter 33 of his *Seventh Book*, Augustine rightly argues that Christianity, the only true religion, "has alone been able to manifest that the gods of the nations are most impure demons, who desire to be thought gods, availing themselves of the names of certain defunct souls, or the appearance of mundane creatures, and with proud impurity divine honors, and envying human souls their conversion to the true God."

The early Church fathers did believe in and preach against satanic forces. They taught the casting out, or exorcism, of demons. They possessed Christ's power to deliver the afflicted from demonic forces.

It is modern theologians who have said little about demon power; I find that the less preachers teach on demons, the more control the devil has over society. The Word of God says, *And the truth shall make you free* (John 8:32).

2. WHAT IS THE SPIRIT OF INFIRMITY AND HOW DOES IT AFFECT A PERSON?

A spirit of infirmity is one of the devil's spirits. There are many types of these spirits, all of which cause sickness. The suffering caused by a spirit of infirmity is not a real physical illness and cannot be detected or treated by a physician.

3. HOW DO YOU TELL WHETHER A PERSON HAS A SPIRIT OF INFIRMITY OR PHYSICAL DEFECT AND IS IT DEMON POSSESSION?

The sickness caused by a spirit of infirmity may move all over the body. It may manifest itself as a backache, then sick headache, or perhaps an upset stomach, or pain in the chest. No treatment is successful against it. No pills or shots bring long-lasting relief from it. No doctor can determine what is wrong with the patient

128

suffering from this malady. In fact, literally millions of people are being sent to psychiatrists by their doctors because the cause of their illness and suffering cannot be found.

Of course, the reason that medical treatment is unsuccessful is because the source of the problem is spiritual. A person being attacked by a spirit of infirmity needs to be set free by the delivering power of Jesus. God wants to set people free from the infirmities of the devil.

I would say that a person with a spirit of infirmity who did not seek deliverance, but surrendered himself to the evil thing in his body, would certainly be moving toward complete domination by Satan. Instead, the sufferer should find a man of God to exercise divine authority and dominion over the devil's power, binding and rebuking the spirit of infirmity.

4.   CAN DEMONS BLESS A PERSON AS WELL AS CURSE HIM?

The devil does not really bless--he pretends or promises to bless. Through spiritism, the devil may convince a person that he has made him well, but that person will become sick again by the power of the devil. A demonic "blessing" is fleeting. Actually, it is a lie in disguise.

The devil is a deceiver. He has no tenderness or compassion toward any human being. If you could visit the countries of the world where demon power is strongest, you would not find people being helped or blessed by demons. Instead, you would find mulitudes of people starving to death and ravaged by disease. Those who are totally demon possessed, who have given themselves over completely to the devil, are treated worst of all.

Demons, which are those angelic beings who fell from heaven with Lucifer, wish to possess human beings for various reasons. First, having no body of their own, they desire a temporal dwelling place. Second, they possess humans in order to strike back at God and His greatest creation, mankind, and oppress and destroy them. The purpose of demons is not to bless man, but to destroy him. In this way they hope to hurt God. The Bible expressly teaches that all good comes from God.

James 1:17, *Every good gift and every perfect gift is from above, and cometh down from the Father. . .*

5.   DO YOU THINK THAT THERE IS A CONNECTION BETWEEN DEMON POWER AND THE SPREADING USE OF THE ADDICTION TO NARCOTICS?

I am absolutely convinced that narcotics are major instruments of the devil's power today. If you remember that Satan is constantly striving to strike at God by attacking and hurting man, you can see how drugs such as heroin, marijuana, amphetamines, and other addictive narcotics fit into this pattern. They bring nothing but misery, heartache, and suffering to every life they touch.

Also, the devil's traditional mode of operation is revealed in the pattern of drug use. People experiment with drugs because they have been promised a thrill, a "kick," an exciting, and a rewarding experience. For some, perhaps, at first it is. But soon the thrill is gone, and they must use more or stronger drugs, until finally they are hopelessly trapped, getting in deeper and deeper every day.

At first, the devil's promise of "good" seems to come true. Then, the whole thing rapidly becomes a hideous nightmare. What started out as a search for a "kick" leads to all sorts of evil--lying, thievery, robbery, lust, prostitution, murder, and anything else required of the addict. How the devil must mock and scorn to have a human so totally in his control!

In the countries of the world where demon power is strongest, you will find thousands of people using drugs. In China, Tibet, India, Indonesia, and other countries, narcotics and strong drugs are used in weird, unearthly worship rituals to demons and idol gods.

I have walked through dark, narrow alleys in Hong Kong littered with the sprawled, emaciated bodies of suffering, dying addicts. The air was so heavy with the smoke and stench of burning opium and hashish that I could hardly get my breath. You could look into the tortured faces and tormented eyes of these people and see that they were demon possessed.

My flesh crawled with the overwhelming sensation of evil. My spirit told me unmistakably that the devil's power was strong all around.

I have seen the same look on the faces of young people in this country who have given themselves over to drugs. You see, drugs take control of the mind and spirit. This allows the devil to move in; it gives him free hand to possess and control a person's entire being.'

Many young people are being deceived and trapped by Satan through narcotics in our country today. Soon they find themselves in the grip of something from which they can't break away. It is more than a physical craving or appetite. It is a spirit!

That's why there is no medical cure for addiction. The addict may seem to be off drugs and perfectly normal, then go berserk for no apparent reason. Addicts need to be delivered and set free from the demonic power of the devil. There is no other cure.

One more thing: the people who push drugs, selling them to youngsters and even the children, are definitely demon-possessed. They know the terrible consequences of their hellish product, yet they entice and seduce others, sometimes innocent people, into partaking of the poison that will ruin their lives. These are the most cruel, most despicable people on the face of the earth. Their action is not normal or natural at all. It is the work of the devil. Their only hope is deliverance from demon power through a man of God with great spiritual power and authority.

6. **I LIVE IN CONSTANT FEAR OF SINNING AGAINST THE HOLY SPIRIT AND OF LOSING MY MIND. COULD THIS FEAR BE A TORMENTING SPIRIT?**

In answer to this question, let me first stress that fear of any type is wrong and is of satanic origin. What we must realize is that the Bible says that the devil is the accuser of the brethren.

Revelation 12:10, *And I heard a loud voice saying in heaven, Now is come salvation, and strength, and the kingdom of our God, and the power of his Christ: for the accuser of our brethren is cast down, which accused them before our God day and night.*

Many people are fearful of sinning against the Holy Spirit when there is no reason for such fear. To sin against the Holy Spirit, a person's total spirit, soul, and body must turn violently against the Bible and hate God.

The second fear, that of losing one's mind, is also one which torments many people unnecessarily. Since God never torments anyone in this way, it is easy to discern that it is Satan who brings such destroying thoughts. As I have stated previously, fear has no rational basis. This is seen very clearly in this case. When you are attacked by fear, you are not losing your mind, neither are you sinning against the Holy Spirit. When that happens, you should obey what the Bible says in James 4:7, *Resist the devil, and he will flee from you.*

A tormenting spirit can only go as far as permitted. It is up to you to take action against it.

Once Rev. Kenneth Hagin, wishing to pray for a person for deliverance, could see a small devil between him and the sick person. This devil was making all kinds of noises and jumping about hysterically, trying to keep Brother Hagin from getting deliverance for the woman. He prayed, "Lord, remove this thing." To which the Lord replied, "**YOU** remove it. **YOU** command it to go." When he did, the spirit was instantly gone and the person for whom he was praying was delivered.

You must not permit the devil to torment you through lies. Our souls are perfectly secure through the blood of Jesus Christ. Paul assures us in 2 Timothy 1:7, . . . *God hath not given us the spirit of fear; but of power, and of love, and of a sound mind.*

You have a divine right to claim a sound mind and certainly God will grant it to you.

131

7.   CAN SUPERSTITION BE AN EVIL SPIRIT?

Superstition thrives under certain conditions. It has to have the proper climate to flourish. Naturally, a spiritually starved and morally bankrupt society produces the best ground for superstition. A man without God turns to superstition for release of tensions and to seek after forbidden knowledge.

Superstition was born because man in his deepest being longs for the supernatural. The soul of man rejects the wholly materialistic way of life. The immortal soul becomes starved for spiritual food when fed philosophy, scientific facts, and religious ritualism. It instinctively seeks release in the unknown. Devoid of truth and life in Christ, foolish and stupid ideas are formed and taught as fact. Mankind seeks after truth.

A man of faith does not inquire of the stars to find God's will for his life. He knows the will of God. He trusts his future to Christ.

The Christian is fully protected from all demon power and from every superstition. Let me list six means of divine protection, as outlined in God's Holy Word, which are available to us as believers:

A.   God's Word is strong armor. The Bible is divine and eternal truth. Therefore, the revealed Word of God possesses power to counteract superstition and to destroy it in every form.

B.   There is security in the shed blood of Christ. Through it Christians have divine power over superstition.

C.   In His Great Commission, our Lord Jesus Christ Himself said that those who believe shall cast out devils.

Mark 16:17, *And these signs shall follow them that believe; In my name shall they cast our devils; they shall speak with new tongues.*

The Christian is secure because of this divine authority invested in him.

D.   I find from my own personal experiences that spiritism and superstition have no place in a Spirit-filled life. Jesus promised us that the Holy Spirit would lead us into all truth.

John 16:13, *Howbeit when he, the Spirit of truth, is come, he will guide you into all truth: for he shall not speak of himself; but whatsoever he shall hear, that shall he speak: and he will shew you things to come.*

Thank God, the blessed Holy Spirit reveals that truth to us and separates it from all error.

E.   Another tremendous safety factor against superstition is the functioning of the gifts of the Holy Spirit in the Church. (1 Corinthians 12). The truth destroys error!

F.   To receive an instantaneous answer to prayer is a miracle. This intimate relationship with God leaves no place for absurd superstitions.

In conclusion, I feel that witchcraft and superstitions are damning powers for a nation or a person.

8.   CAN PEOPLE WHO ARE IN THE FIRST FIVE STAGES OF POS-SESSION BE SET FREE AND IS THE PROCEEDURE THE SAME?

Yes, it is exactly the same. People can also set themselves free in the first stages of demon possession or oppression. When you realize that you are sad or depressed all the time, recognize that it is the devil who is doing it to you. You can just rebel against sadness by saying, "I'm going to have joy. I'm going to have it right now, and I thank God for it." Then start laughing and claim the joy!

9.   CAN A BORN-AGAIN, SPIRIT-FILLED CHRISTIAN WORK IN BARS AND CLUBS SERVING DRINKS? ISN'T IT SATAN WHO CREEPS IN AND DECEIVES SUCH PEOPLE INTO THINKING THAT IT IS ALL RIGHT TO DO SO, THAT THEY CAN WITNESS FOR JESUS WHILE SERVING DRINKS?

I think that you have the answer right there. Dear Christian, never let the devil fool you in this way. When you're in his territory, he's the captain. You had better get back to where Jesus is the Captain. Don't play around with the devil. Anytime you go to a negative place, thinking you're going to do good there, the devil has deceived you.

10.   IS DELIVERANCE OF A CITY THE SAME AS A PERSONAL DELIVERANCE?

My wife labored in Argentina for about eight years. She can tell you that it was one of the hardest places in the world to preach. Many people preached there for years with almost no results. Then a Bible school group began to fast and pray. As they fasted and prayed, they felt a great deliverance.

Evidently they had an experience in this prayer meeting of casting down a power--almost like the one I had in Manila--but with a city rather than a person. When they cast down that power, tremendous revival came to Argentina. It was so mighty that I understand that a million people were saved in one revival meeting. The battle of the world is spiritual. You have to believe that.

11. HOW CAN YOU HELP A PERSON STAY FREE WHEN YOU CANNOT BE WITH HIM; FOR EXAMPLE, A PERSON IN A MENTAL HOSPITAL?

I would think that in the first moment of the release of pressure you would bring him out of that place. He needs to be away from the negative influence inside that institution. It's bad. There's no faith there.

Then he will need to have the Word of God read to him, to be in really spiritual services, to be taught to sing choruses, and to pray--almost as you would teach a baby--to bring him into spiritual depth and blessing. If he doesn't walk in the fullness, he won't have any means of remaining free.

Above all, start quoting the promises of God to him. Sustain him with that strength.

12. PLEASE EXPOUND ON THE DANGERS OF MODERN MUSIC AND DANCE PREVALENT IN OUR SOCIETY TODAY AND THEIR RELATIONSHIP TO SATANIC BONDAGE.

I read about some film makers who were shooting a film in Africa. They had just started playing the music for the film when one of the tribal people came to them and said, "I wouldn't play that music if I were you."

"Why not?" asked the film crew.

"Well," responded the tribesmen, "I don't know where you got it, but that is the music we use to call up the dead spirits to worship them."

The modern world has gone to the pagan, heathen peoples and brought back the offbeat and hardbeat rhythms they use. Without knowing it, many of our young people today are worshipping the devil. There is mounting evidence now proving that heavy metal rock music has invaded the youth culture, bringing young people into a realm of unspeakable horror. The music is bizarre, the words take the listener on a roller-coaster ride straight to Hades.

If you pick up the devil's music and start singing it and playing it, you're involving yourself with hell. I would say that any kind of music which tears up a person's insides the way rock music does, destroys spiritual strength and power. Young people who constantly play it at an ear-splitting level until it pounds into their brains, show that they are already very close to possession. Keep your mind strong and alert and controlled--keep it on Jesus.

13. PLEASE COMMENT ON THE ADDICTION TO TELEVISION AND OTHER DIVERSIONS THAT WOULD BE A DISTRACTION TO THE CHRISTIAN WALK.

In Germany and in England recently a certain society gave three hundred families in each of these countries a certain amount of money every week for a period of thirteen weeks if they would allow their TV sets to be sealed up. They were actually paid not to watch television. Then these people were monitored by psychologists and sociologists to determine the effects of TV withdrawal upon them.

In a very short while, many of these people went into some sort of delirium tremens. Finally not one single family could stand it. They became so nervous and neurotic that they actually began to shake. They were like drug addicts. They had to have their daily "fix" of television.

Probably 95 percent of what is on television is bad. There is always a love scene in every show and usually it is a dirty love scene. How could you have faith in doctors after seeing how they are depicted on the tube with every doctor playing around with someone else's wife?

Television has no relationship with reality at all. It is just one big lie. If a person is going to drink in all that junk, it will have an effect upon him. There is no way around it. The only answer for a Christian is to turn off that type of program and not allow it into his house. We must guard our minds and spirits and those of our children against the devastating effects of TV's distorted portrayal of life.

14. WHERE DID JESUS DIRECT THE DEMONIC SPIRITS TO GO?

First of all, don't misdirect them. For example, if you should say to a spirit, "Go back to hell from whence you came," he won't even come out because he hasn't gone to hell yet. He's one of the fallen spirits that fell from heaven with Satan. They have not yet been incarcerated in hell. At the end of the age, they will be bound there forever with Satan, but not until then. They're not in hell. If you tell them to go back to hell, they will know that you don't understand what you're doing, and they won't obey you at all.

One time the Lord Jesus permitted some spirits to go into a herd of pigs. That was the only time we know of that he allowed such a thing.

I don't know if it's really important to tell them where to go. I just command them to come out. If I do send them somewhere, I will say, "Go into the void of space, into the emptiness of space." That's out of the way of human beings.

15. **ARE FETISHES AND EMBLEMS USED IN JEWELRY CONSIDERED EMBLEMS OF DEMON POWER?**

Yes. I wouldn't have one around whether it is made in this country or elsewhere. Have nothing to do with anything connected with demon power.

16. **SINCE EVERYTHING IN HEAVEN IS PURE AND GOOD, HOW COULD LUCIFER LIVE THERE AND BECOME PROUD AND START ALL THE EVIL WHICH IS IN THE WORLD?**

Evil does not begin on the outside; it begins in the heart. Lucifer looked in the mirror and said, "You are the most beautiful one here. You should be above everything else, including God." He should have resisted those thoughts, but instead he conceived them, brought them to birth, and acted upon them. Evil can come in the sweetest of places if it is allowed to generate inside a person.

17. **JAMES 4:7 SAYS, *SUBMIT YOURSELVES THEREFORE TO GOD. RESIST THE DEVIL, AND HE WILL FLEE FROM YOU.* HOW CAN WE SUBMIT OURSELVES TO GOD?**

Submitting ourselves to God can have to do with our business, our domestic lives, and our own spiritual lives. To submit to God means to give oneself fully on a daily basis to the Lord in all these areas. We should submit ourselves to the Word of God and do what it says.

18. **A RELATIVE OF MINE SAYS THAT HE BELIEVES IN GOD, BUT HE IS A HINDU. IS HINDUISM DEVIL WORSHIP?**

Hindu gods are spirits. If your relative is attached to a Hindu deity, and most likely he is, that deity is an evil spirit. If he is worshipping that deity and if he has a mantra (a secret word that he receives from a guru and which he keeps repeating inside), that is an open door for the devil. By putting his mind in neutral, which is what the mantra accomplishes, evil spirits can enter in through the unguarded door to his mind.

In a way, all heathens are under the oppression of the devil because they have believed a lie. Hindus have over 300 million gods, so everything is a god--and that is not truth. There is only one God--and that one God has one Son, the Lord Jesus. There is one Holy Spirit who comes forth from the Father and the Son to bless us and walk with us.

19. HOW CAN A LYING SPIRIT AND A LUSTFUL SPIRIT BE CAST OUT OF A FAMILY?

God will not make anyone live right. For instance, He did not make Adolf Hitler live right. We are free moral agents who can choose to go to heaven or hell. If this man does not want to serve God, he won't serve and love Him, and he won't love his family. All you can do is pray that the devil's power will be broken from his life. He must want to be free from the spirits that bind him before he can be free. He cannot be free by your wanting him to be free.

NOTES

Bringing Quality Education To Your Home

In the last several years, educators around the country, including all of us here at Indiana Chr
University, have seen a definite new trend in education. More and more, education is becoming d
tralized and less campus-focused. This trend seems to be true in all areas of education, and espe
in college work.

We here at ICU are very thankful that God has allowed us to be more than trend observers; we
been trendsetters. Because of his vision, insight and forethought--or should we say "prophetic k
edge"--Dr. Lester Sumrall developed a Bible curriculum which we can offer to the world through a
correspondence studies and video extension campuses. Due to his continuous travels as an eva
list and missionary during the years that he was trying to obtain his college education, Dr. Su
became acutely aware of the fact that traditional campus-based education would prove increas
impractical for a greater number of people as their lives became more and more mobile. With this
insight, Dr. Sumrall worked tirelessly to produce a college system that could go with the student r
than demanding that the student abandon his mission for a period of years to be anchored to a
The result was an off-campus program that makes Indiana Christian University literally a school v
global campus.

This correspondence program has allowed us to provide degree programs to ministers who ca
leave their churches, housewives who must stay with their families, missionaries in isolated mi
posts, inmates in correctional institutions, patients in long-term medical facilities--and the list go
and on.

In breaking beyond the limitation of our walls, ICU has begun to fulfill not only Dr. Sumrall's
date, but also the directive left to us by Jesus Christ Himself: "Go ye therefore, and teach all natio
(Matthew 28:19).

Introducing Indiana Christian University

Indiana Christian University is an independent school of higher learning serving all religiou
nominations. The student body and faculty reflect various types of church backgrounds, rather tha
one denomination. The university is incorporated in the state of Indiana and grants degrees to
who satisfactorily complete the prescribed course of study.

The school's history dates to 1907, when a group of Christian people formed an institution for t
ing the Bible and Bible-related subjects. It was chartered in the state of Indiana in 1923 as In
Bible Institute, becoming Indiana Bible College in 1934. The present name was adopted in 194

In addition to training ministers and professional people, the school has helped thousands of
tian laypeople gain a greater understanding of the Bible and has prepared them for Christian life

I

e part of the Lester Sumrall Evangelistic Association in 1988. In 1990, the school was relocated
idianapolis to its present home in South Bend. A merger with the former World Harvest Bible
e was finalized in 1993, resulting in two campuses: Indianapolis and South Bend.

Programs of Study

ertificate of Achievement in Charismatic Studies is awarded to students who successfully com-
ie basic curriculum of charismatic studies with a grade average of 2.00 (C) or better. The basic
Jum includes: Faith, English, Christian Foundations, The Total Man, Human Illness and Divine
ϳ, Demon Power, The Gifts of the Holy Spirit, Prayer, and four hours of Practicum.

Associate of Arts in Christian Ministry and Bachelor of Arts in Christian Ministry are awarded to
ts who:

Demonstrate a Christian character which the school can recommend.

Complete the prescribed course (56 credit hours for the Associate of Arts in Christian Ministry
program; 112 credit hours for the Bachelor of Arts in Christian Ministry program) with a grade
average of 2.00 (C) or better.

	Associate of Arts in Christian Ministry	Bachelor of Arts in Christian Ministry
age Department		
ɹlish	3 hrs.	3 hrs.
Department		
Testament	6 hrs.	16 hrs.
v Testament	6 hrs.	16 hrs.
gy Department-must include	21 hrs.	21 hrs.
courses listed for the		
ificate program		
y Department		
cticum	8 hrs.	16 hrs.
Department	3 hrs.	6 hrs.
es	9 hrs.	34 hrs.

Earn College Credit
For This Course Through

1. Complete the application process.

    a) Complete and mail the application form along with the $25 application fee.

    b) Request your high school and/or college(s) to mail transcripts to ICU.

    c) Give the Pastor's Reference Form to your pastor and request that it be returned directly to

    d) In order to request consideration for life experience for practicum credits, submit a full res
        showing dates of ministry and full responsibilities involved. Verification from an overseer
        other recognizable authority must accompany each ministry assignment.

2. Upon acceptance you will receive:

    a) a transcript indicating any coursework which has been transferred from previous institutio
        life experience.

    b) a study plan indicating the ICU courses recommended to complete the program of study
        are enrolling into. Be sure to keep this guideline and follow it carefully.

    c) a registration form for registering for your courses.

    d) a Sumrall Publications catalog for ordering your class study materials and tapes.

    e) a "How to Write a Term Paper" manual.

3. Complete the registration form and return it along with the appropriate fee to ICU.

4. Complete the order form for your class study materials and tapes and return it along with the
    proper payment to Sumrall Publishing.

5. When your class study materials and tapes arrive, read the lessons and listen to the tapes in
    way most helpful to you. It is suggested that you read the lesson once, listen to the tape, and
    read the lesson again. Complete the test which will be mailed to you upon the submission of
    class registration. Carefully following the instructions in the term paper manual, write and sub
    term paper on a topic related to the course. The paper should be 10-12 double-spaced, type
    ten pages. Font size should not exceed 14 points and margins should not exceed 1 1/2 inch
    All information from source material must be properly footnoted and listed in a bibliography.